MUSINGS *of a* MEDIOCRE GARDENER

Dedicated to my husband, Rob
and my son, Andrew
and to my parents, Dorothy and Joe Dana
and to all those
who work in food pantries and homeless shelters,
who make life better for others

MUSINGS *of a* MEDIOCRE GARDENER

DORI DANA HUDSON

CHALICE
PRESS
ST. LOUIS, MISSOURI

Cover image: Getty Images
Interior art: © Art Parts
Cover and interior design: Elizabeth Wright

Visit Chalice Press on the World Wide Web at
www.chalicepress.com

10 9 8 7 6 5 4 3 2 1   06 07 08 09 10

Library of Congress Cataloging–in–Publication Data

Hudson, Dori Dana.
  Musings of a mediocre gardener / Dori Dana Hudson.
    p. cm.
  ISBN-13: 978-0-8272-2333-2 (pbk. : alk. paper)
  ISBN-10: 0-8272-2333-1 (pbk. : alk. paper)
  1. Gardening—Religious aspects—Christianity. 2. Gardens—
Religious life. I. Title.
  BV4596.G36H83 2006
  242—dc22

                                                    2005025662

Printed in the United States of America

contents

prelude

This book is an enigma, a librarian's nightmare. It's about gardening, but it offers no tips or "how-tos." It's about vegetables, flowers, and weeds, but it's really about ideas. It's about my life, but it is not an autobiography. It tells a story, but only in pieces. It's spiritual, but not really religious. I like to think that this book is about faithful living. A friend called it "a book about life choices." I like that description, and I hope you will too.

Originally this book was just thirty musings. I had decided to begin a prayer journal. However, when I sat down to begin, I found myself making a list of thoughts about the garden that summer. I began to write and didn't stop for three weeks. Thus the first season was born.

My first idea was to make copies for my family only, but with the miracle of computers and copy machines, it was easy to make copies. And so I started to give them away. In that simple way, the booklet's ministry began, as more and more copies went out.

With the next two growing seasons, I found myself again writing down thoughts that had come to me in the garden. Each season had a distinctive character and different musings, resulting in three booklets, and more and more copies went out.

I am thrilled and blessed that Chalice Press has chosen to offer this book with all three seasons under one title so that more and more people may share them. With hope that God may use my words again, I offer these musings as a mediocre gardener.

Shalom,
Dori Dana Hudson

first season

Springtime

Today is the first day when the weather hints of tilting from cold to warm. I can feel in my soul the stirring of spring and the deep urging to plant. I sense this urging is somehow born of very ancient instincts, but I also know it comes from my childhood.

When I was growing up, our family had a large garden in the backyard. In the summer, much of our family life revolved around the garden, and the garden became a source of pride. We treated anyone who came to our home in the summer to a tour of the garden. My parents were both fine gardeners, placing the tending of the garden high on their list of priorities. I have never been, nor do I wish to be, as knowledgeable or as attentive as they. I am content to plant and let the natural processes produce the harvest. I am content to be a mediocre gardener.

Yet every spring, Rob and I plant. Planting has its own special joy, quite separate from the harvest. I feel I would plant even if there were no harvest. Indeed, in Vermont we planted a garden shortly before moving. Planting is a chance to touch the earth and see it respond. It is a chance to be part of God's great creation.

Planting has become for us a time of celebration. In Kentucky, we established a family tradition of planting our small garden on Easter, as a symbol of resurrection. In Illinois, we gathered family and friends to plant on May Day, my birthday.

Planting is indeed a celebration of God's desire to renew the earth and renew our lives. Planting is for us a celebration of the promise of another year to come.

Gift of the Ground

Our hunger garden began when we bought this house. Attached to this house for decades has been an extra lot across the alley. In that lot are an ancient apple tree, a blackberry patch, a half-dozen young peach and cherry trees, and a huge garden about 45 feet by 50 feet.

The first year we planted only about one-fourth of the garden plot. We loaned one-fourth to a neighbor. The rest simply went to waste...and weeds. Still, we soon found ourselves with produce to spare. Determined not to freeze and can—which I loathe—we began giving the vegetables away to neighbors, both those we knew and those who were strangers. Finally, we took some vegetables to our local food pantry. There we were surprised to learn that the pantry rarely had fresh vegetables to give away. Amazed, we realized that here was a ministry literally in our own back yard!

The next spring we planted the entire 2250–square-foot garden. Our only confidence came from knowing, first, that this ground had been a garden for at least four decades and, second, that God has given to Illinois some of the richest soil in the world. As Rob says, "In Illinois, you just stick it in the ground, and it grows." In addition to feeding us, the earth generously gave about 1000 pounds of food to be passed on to those who are hungry.

It was an abundance to give, a special joy we had not known before. As people of modest means, we will never be major financial donors to a cause; but here with our hunger garden we had the chance to give richly and make a difference.

Tilling

I love the day we get our garden tilled. We all stand outside watching the man as his big machine digs deeply into the dirt. Tangled stalks and decomposing leaves, skeletons of the past season, disappear into the ground. The garden is ready for a new beginning, ready to receive the seeds and plants.

We are willing to pay to have the garden tilled professionally. It saves time, energy, and a lot of sore muscles. Plus, it immediately readies the ground for the task we enjoy best—planting. Our tilling man worked well past dark and then stated his fee. Shocked at his price I argued with him and then simply paid him almost double what he asked. Tilling has a great value for us.

As adults and marriage partners, we must recognize what each of us values. When one says, "I can't afford it," what he or she means is, "It does not have this much value for me." We all choose what we can and can't afford.

Several years ago we realized we were always asking about contributions, "How much can we afford?" We meant, "How much money do we have left over?" We had put giving at the bottom of our priorities, so the donations we made lacked joy and generosity. We decided to restate our values, to tithe our income, and to dedicate the first portion of our money for contributions. We chose a monthly target amount from which to make donations. Giving then became certain, fun, and essential.

I paid the tilling man more than he asked because tilling is something we value. Like tilling, tithing is something we value and find worth paying for.

Jerie

It's Saturday, and soon my friend Jerie will be out in the garden. She has come faithfully every Saturday this spring to help us plant and weed. Her presence has made weeding an act of friendship. It's a friendship bonded by talk while bending to a common task.

Jerie goes to our church, but I knew her only in passing. Last year we put a request for gardening help in the church newsletter but got no response. This spring Jerie tentatively inquired whether we planned to plant a hunger garden again, and did we still want help. The seed planted a year before had borne fruit.

Jerie is a valuable friend in part because she lives down the alley and around the corner. Like us, she has chosen to live in this neighborhood. This neighborhood is not affluent; this is the poor, under-educated, under-employed northeast corner of Springfield. This is a neighborhood of many problems, but it is a neighborhood that allows us to live cheaply. That, in turn, allows me to pursue my art, Rob to work for the homeless shelter, and both of us to have time and resources to parent Andrew.

However, when domestic violence erupts in the family to one side or the police arrest the teenager to the other side, we wonder about our choice. Then it helps to remember that Jerie—caring, quiet, well-educated, gentle Jerie—shares our choice of neighborhood. When you seek to walk a less-traveled path, it is helpful to know that a few others are walking there too.

Radishes

I love radishes. They are bright red and round and smooth. They add bite to a salad without leaving an aftertaste, or they are just fun to crunch by themselves. When I eat lunch alone, I often have three or four radishes as if they were a secret special treat.

But I love radishes best as a gardener. The little round seeds are fun to plant, and then they are the very first crop to pop out of the ground and give the promise of a new creation. They are also the first harvest of the garden. I feel I am in the ancient tradition of offering to God the "first fruits" as I take our first bowl of radishes over to the food pantry. There are always delighted exclamations of, "Look! Dori and Andrew are here with radishes. Don't they look wonderful! Let's clear off this table and make it our table for fresh vegetables!" Then with waves and the parting good-byes, they say, "Thanks so much. We'll see you again soon!" What they mean is—we will see you again soon with broccoli, beans, tomatoes, peppers, squash...and more radishes.

Radishes, my thank-offering to God, are a promise of things to come.

White Radishes 1

This year our seeds from the Hunger Coalition included several plain brown envelopes marked radishes. We planted them. When they began to grow, we realized we had three different varieties of radishes: two red and one white. The red ones ripened as expected, one a little earlier than the other. Andrew and April, his playmate from next door, would eagerly run into the house asking, "Can we pick some radishes?" I'd hand him a bowl, and out to the garden they would dash. The red radishes come up easily. The kids can snap off the tops, fill the bowl quickly, and run to show what they have done.

Unfortunately, this is not the case with the white radishes. They have tops as prickly as cactus. You must use gloves and long sleeves, and even then expect to get scratched. Plus, once having gripped the plant, you must pull hard as they hold tenaciously to the ground and often snap in two rather than yield up the whole root. Exasperated, we have given up harvesting them and have left them in the ground, asking, "Who would ever knowingly plant white radishes!?!"

Not all that we plant in our lives will turn out as we hope. Each of us must face hard times and heartaches and dead ends. We may be tempted to wish we had never embarked on a new way. But if we only plant that which we know well, that which we are sure will grow to our expectations, then we will never venture out to find new experiences or to choose a new path. A new venture may result in prickles and scratches—it may be a white radish—but it also may reveal a rich harvest that God has in store for us.

Horseradish

This morning I was fuming again over the white radishes—too prickly to pick, too spicy to eat. I was complaining to Rob that the red radishes were almost all gone, and our whole row of white ones was useless.

As I was talking, I pulled things out of the refrigerator for lunch. Let's see—leftover pizza for Andrew and hot dogs for Rob and me. Three plates, knives, forks, and spoons. Apple sauce, leftover salad, and three milks. Oh yes, mustard and relish for Rob, and ketchup and horseradish for me. *Horseradish*?! Could it be that our too prickly, too spicy, exasperating radishes are really horseradishes?

I tried to find out. I looked in my cookbooks and my gardening catalogs, but couldn't find the answer. I still don't know. You may be tempted to say, "Is it really important to find out?" Well, it is to me, because horseradish holds a distinct, special place in my refrigerator. You see, I am the only one who likes horseradish; Rob and Andrew both hate it.

I am a caregiver by temperament. When I go to a garage sale, I look first at the children's clothes, then at the men's clothes. If I still have time and money, I glance through the women's things. I love Christmastime because it is a time to choose presents for others. That is my nature.

But now I am trying to learn to take time for myself, to take walks and read books, to pray and meditate. I am learning of my need to renew my energy, refresh my patience, and to restore my soul. Horseradish reminds me of that need because I buy it just for me.

White Radishes 2

Today, I remembered my query about who would ever plant white radishes. Today, perhaps I found the answer.

For now it is fall, and as I was picking tomatoes, I happened by our patch of deserted white radishes. Now the roots are two to three inches in diameter, and stick four to five inches out of the ground. I can only guess how far down they may go. As I looked at them today, I realized that my disdain is modern, born of grocery stores and refrigerators. Were I a cave woman gathering food for the winter, I would be overjoyed to see these radishes. I would know they were good to eat, spicy but not bitter, and I would know they would last till spring. Joyfully, I would dig up a big basketful and be thankful for having a whole row of radishes to feed my family after the cold weather sets in and food becomes scarce.

Today, I felt gratitude for all that God has provided for my life and my family. Today, I even lifted up thanks for those exasperating white radishes.

Early Morning

It's 7:45 a.m., time for Rob to head for work and time for me to come in from the garden. Today was one of those spring mornings when it is wonderful to be out in the garden early. I got up stealthily, slipped into my garden clothes, and headed out into the quiet. The morning air seemed so fresh, the sunlight was still soft, and the birds were raising a joyful chorus. As I worked with my hands, I had time to think and get composed for the day. Plus, I had time to listen, to feel, to receive wholeness, and to be in God's presence.

I don't get up early every morning. I believe my days would go more smoothly if I did. But most mornings I sleep till Rob wakes me up to say, "Good-bye," or until Andrew comes in to bounce on me. Perhaps I sleep because it's a lazy habit. I have found in my life that good habits are as hard to make as bad habits are to break—maybe harder. So I sleep away many early mornings.

But maybe I sleep for a deeper reason. Early morning was the time I used to call and talk to my mother, and it is early morning when her memory is strongest with me. If I sleep late, I must then hurry and don't have time to think or feel or face that sorrow. But today, the morning was so sweet that I feel far more rested for having gotten up early. My mother seemed near, and I am comforted, not sad...I hope that I will get up early again tomorrow.

Sun

It's only 9:00 in the morning, but the July sun has driven me inside from the garden. I'm hot and sweaty; and, despite my big sun hat, I feel kind of dizzy. I'm really ready to get in the shower and leave the garden for another day.

As I stand in the shower with cool water pouring over me, an image of a vegetable field in the Rio Grande Valley fills my mind. I've lived in Texas, where it is even hotter and the sun even more relentless than here in Illinois. In my mind I see the migrant workers bending to their task of picking the vegetables. Although they may have started at dawn, I know they will not be allowed to stop at 9:00 a.m. It will be many, long hours before they can rest for the day. Even then, it is not likely they will have a nice, cool shower to wash away the dirt and the sweat and the prickles. No wonder migrant workers age so rapidly.

Tomorrow when I go to the grocery and pick up a watermelon or some oranges or a head of lettuce, let me remember the sweat of others that has brought it to me. Let me serve it with the reverence and gratitude it deserves.

Rain

It is raining again today, as it has at least once a week all summer long. In fact, we have not needed to water since we planted. The whole summer has been hot and wet—seemingly perfect weather for growing things. Indeed, the plants have really grown. The squash plants are five feet in diameter, the pepper plants are three feet tall, and the tomatoes are a mass, despite my suckering them. Were I growing leaves and stems, this would be a record year!

But the odd thing is that the squash plants, the pepper plants, and the tomato plants—for all their glory—have produced comparatively little fruit. The peppers are small. The tomatoes have crusty spots and have to be picked green because they burst if left to ripen. And the squash are few, and molding before becoming big enough to harvest.

All of this reminds me of Jesus' saying, "Truly I tell you, it will be hard for a rich person to enter the kingdom of heaven" (Mt. 19:23). Sometimes riches, like plentiful rain, make us so concentrate our energies on ourselves that we grow lush, green, interesting lives, but bear little fruit. It may be that we can only be compassionate if we have known sorrow, only be generous if we have known financial stress, only be comforting if we have known worry, only be helpful if we have known need, and only be joyful if we have known depression…It may be that we can only be bountiful if we have known some drought.

Hot Chili Peppers

One crop has been abundant this year: the small, hot chili peppers. We had not planned to grow hot peppers, but the plants arrived from the Hunger Coalition along with our bell peppers. I planted them thinking that they might help deter some of the insects, as do marigolds, nasturtiums, and garlic.

Now we have oodles of hot chili peppers; I'd say enough to keep a Mexican restaurant going for a year! My neighbor Dan suggested we string them up to dry as kitchen decorations. I thought maybe we could make a garland for the Christmas tree, or maybe we could varnish them and make necklaces. After all, chilies aren't really nutritional, are they? Their role is just one of flavor and decoration—right?!?

Well today I was again thinking about the abundant hot peppers, and it occurred to me the only reason I do not value them is because I have a refrigerator in my kitchen and a freezer in my basement. In much of the world, food is made spicy to preserve it. Meat cooked with chilies will not spoil as quickly, despite the high heat of Mexico, Senegal, India, or Thailand. The presence of hot spices in food is not an accident or a matter of cultural tradition. It is essential to nutrition. So perhaps it is all part of God's wondrous plan that during seasons of less food production, the hot chilies will be bountiful to preserve what little food there is.

Yellow Bell Peppers

Today I found a yellow pepper. Excitedly I picked it and brought it into the house. I love yellow and red bell peppers. They are so sweet and delicious to eat. However, I seldom buy yellow or red bell peppers in the store. They look so lush and tempting, but boast a price far higher than green peppers. Surprisingly, a yellow or red bell pepper is like a brother, or a cousin, to the green bell pepper, only it has been bred to ripen. Given the right conditions, green peppers will also ripen to red or yellow.

So why not let green peppers ripen? Well, because often they rot while they are still green. Then they are no good, and so we pick peppers green. That has been particularly true this year when we had so much rain. The pepper plants are big and lush and green, but the bell peppers themselves are scarce. Other years, the peppers have been so numerous that their weight knocked over the plants, tomato cages and all. That is not true this year. This year the peppers are few, and in order not to waste any, I have picked them green. Only this one pepper, hidden way down in the weeds and covered from my view by leaves, has turned yellow and sweet.

It makes me think about people and friendships. Often I try to make friends with those who are most visible, the outgoing and the busy ones. Often I am disappointed because those I meet have too little time for me, and our friendship never ripens. I think that I need to look more deeply into the shadows for the person who is hidden from view, a person who has time and desire to let our friendship grow sweet.

Weeds

I wish we were growing weeds. I could have the very best crop on the block. Weeds are so high-spirited, so relentless, so eternally optimistic. They never give up.

In the spring when the weather is pleasant and you want to spend hours in the garden, it is very rewarding to battle the weeds. We pull them up at every turn. We put down black plastic between the rows to block them from the light. We carefully mulch around our plants.

But, come the heat of summer and the beginning of the harvest, it takes nearly all of our shortened gardening time to simply pick the vegetables. The weeds begin to find their way through the mulch, around the plastic, and next to our plants. Then, in July, we go away on vacation. When we return, the garden is a giant weed patch.

Today as I looked out over the weeds, I tried to tell myself that some research suggests you should let the weeds grow in July to provide alternative food for the annual influx of insects. I find solace in that research because I know in my heart that midsummer weeding will never be included in my priorities of things to do. Not weeding is part of being a mediocre gardener. Of course, if the weeds really bothered me, I could choose to grow only a small garden, one where I could keep the weeds at bay. Or I could feel so overwhelmed by the weeds that I would grow no garden at all. Instead, I choose to keep my giant weed patch that steadily yields baskets of fresh food for the hungry.

Crabgrass

Of all the weeds, crabgrass is the most contentious and astonishing to me. In a perverse way, I admit great admiration for it. God created it to multiply rapidly, either through putting out shoots that root, or through seeds that spout almost instantly. It will grow anywhere it finds sunlight, in places with almost no soil at all. Each spring, we put black plastic between the rows to keep down the weeds. Over the summer, dirt washes over the plastic, and we find crabgrass growing in that thin layer of soil.

Fighting crab grass is much like fighting violence in our American society. We don't buy weapon toys, we don't own a Nintendo™, and we restrict the use of television. We even stopped watching the news because it was too violent (for Rob and me, as well as for Andrew). Still violence persists. "Good" movies have fighting, and books from the library depict kids using their fists. Even if we were able to keep all violence out of our home, the only way to keep it out of Andrew's life would be to totally isolate him from other kids. Going to a friend's home is a wonderful chance to play with toys we don't allow. Going to school means confronting kids who think it is fun to pick on others.

Like crabgrass, violence just keeps poking up. The only thing I know to do about crabgrass is to keep pulling it up.

The only thing I know to do about violence is keep listening and explaining and showing another way. We are hoping that this will help Andrew choose nonviolent ways when he is old enough to make his own choices.

Carrots

I don't think we'll plant carrots again. They are too much work! First, we mixed sand into the soil before we sprinkled the tiny seed. The seedlings came up slowly and grew small and weak. We spent many hours trying to rid the carrots of the morning glories and crabgrass that threatened to strangle them. I like to weed by the handfuls, but in order not to pull up the delicate carrots, we had to weed by the pinch. It was tedious work.

Now at long last, it is time to harvest the carrots. However, they must be dug with a shovel, for they cannot be pulled. The carrots are muddy and knobby and strong in flavor. Every once in a while, we find a rotten carrot. Few things in my world are as revolting as a slimy, stinky, rotten carrot! This morning Jerie and I were digging carrots. After quite an effort, we had hardly any harvest. I was complaining and ready to quit. I also was convinced that I never wanted to see another carrot plant again.

Then life pulled a trick on me. Jerie started to dig up a plant that was in flower. I said, "Is that a carrot? It looks like a Queen Anne's lace." She laughed and said, "I think they are about the same plant. I'm pretty sure if you leave these carrots in the ground, they will bloom each year and look like Queen Anne's lace."

I was dumbfounded! I love Queen Anne's lace; it is my favorite wildflower. I even carried it in my wedding bouquet. Could this lovely flower really be related to this annoying vegetable? Could this be God's way of telling me to be careful with my scorn...that nothing (and no one) is without redemptive qualities?

Tomatoes

Today Andrew and I delivered a large load of tomatoes to the food pantry. As I moved the tomatoes from my laundry baskets to the table, I sorted them. I set aside any that had split open because they were slightly overripe. I took out those that one of God's small creatures had nibbled on. In all I sorted out about a dozen tomatoes, which I returned to the basket to bring home. On reaching home, I shared my blemished tomatoes with my neighbor Karen and put the rest in our refrigerator. They wait there to be sliced, or sauced, or sent to the compost pile.

Why do I sort them? It is simply that I know that imperfect tomatoes will be passed over. They will be left to spoil and be thrown away at the food pantry. It seems a paradox of our affluent society that people who are hungry will be choosy about food given to them free. Many will not accept a tomato that is largely good, but has a spot that must be cut out.

It angers me to think of all the perfectly good food that is thrown away in America because it is slightly flawed. It makes me wonder, "Do we also throw away people who are slightly flawed?" It saddens me that Americans are taught to expect perfection: a perfection that really means similarity. We talk about diversity, but do we affirm in others—or ourselves—bumpy, slightly-chewed-on, or split-open characteristics?

It maddens me about the tomatoes, but then I remember that just because a mother is poor does not mean that she doesn't want her family to have the best. Is it a mark of personal pride to only choose the perfect tomatoes, even when they are free?

Cherry Tomatoes

Three summers ago, I thought it would be fun to grow some cherry tomatoes, and I happily bought some plants from the nursery. I was really pleased when they grew quickly and blossomed. Early in the summer, long before the other tomatoes, we had ripe, juicy, cherry tomatoes.

But then the hot weather settled in, and the cherry tomatoes became more and more tedious to pick. Furthermore, the cherry tomato plants continued to grow and spread, intertwining and overwhelming the other tomatoes. We soon learned that our cherry tomatoes were a menace, strangling out their neighbors; and we began to chop them off.

The next summer we were pleased to discover that we had many volunteer tomato plants. We carefully tended them and even transplanted some of them. Every single volunteer plant was a cherry tomato! This year we pulled up every volunteer tomato we could find, and still we have a few cherry tomatoes climbing up and over and smothering our other tomatoes. I wonder how long we will battle them, and I rue the day I brought home these "weeds."

Some decisions in life are like my cherry tomatoes. What seems like a simple, harmless, or fun choice may grow into a bad habit that we have difficulty changing. Most addictions begin innocently, or with a sense of trying something daring— just once. Just as cherry tomatoes become weeds, we must guard ourselves against the little decisions that can grow to be bad habits…grow to be weeds in our lives.

Prickles

Today I tried to get Andrew to help me pick tomatoes. I used every tactic: I asked; I pleaded; I promised to play afterwards; I even tried bribery. But it was to no avail. Oh, he did try. With each new appeal, he would gingerly approach the tomato plants, stepping high to avoid the weeds, pick a few tomatoes, and then call out, "Mom, I'm stuck! Come get me out of here!" Finally, he said, "Mom, I can't help. It's too prickly!" The tomatoes are prickly, the crabgrass does tickle, the mosquitoes do bite, and the grasshoppers do startle; but I still want him to help, and I feel frustrated.

Then I remember my own childhood, and how I hated to work in the garden once July and August came. It was too prickly, hot, scratchy, and scary. Several years ago, my mother commented with delighted amazement in her voice, "I never thought any of my children would have a garden. You all hated to work in the garden. Now, all four of you have gardens!"

As I fuss at Andrew for his unwillingness to do the jobs that I assign him and as I worry he will grow up not knowing the value of work, I need to remember: I, too, hated housework, hid when the dishes needed doing, and didn't want to interrupt my play to set the table. Only as I have created my own home have I valued the responsibility, have I desired to do the mundane, and have I found satisfaction in the completed task.

Only as an adult have I learned to ignore the prickles to gain the harvest.

Black Garden Shoes

This morning I couldn't find my garden shoes. It's muddy outside, so no other shoes will do. I must have my old, black, no-laces sneakers. These are my black garden shoes. When I was a child, my mother had black garden shoes. They were old, black, no-laces sneakers that sat at the back door waiting to be slipped into and out of. When I bought my black sneakers, I didn't intend for them to be garden shoes; but they seemed to migrate of their own accord to the back door, and most often they appear covered with mud and grass clippings. They are just right as garden shoes.

Much of my gardening is like my black garden shoes: unplanned, unstudied, almost instinctive. I don't remember learning to garden. I do remember being out in the garden with my Dad every spring, helping to put the seeds and the plants in the ground. I don't remember learning, but when it comes to planting the lettuce or the beans, I just seem to know.

An article about the unconscious heritage women have from their mothers struck a very familiar chord with me. I worry about what I am patterning into the unconscious of my child. I hope I am modeling kindness, affection, generosity, and concern for others. I hope these will be ingrained in Andrew. But, I regret that I have also left impressions of frustration and anger. I can only wait and pray that the balance will be tipped to the positive.

Who knows? Maybe someday Andrew will have a pair of old, black, no-laces sneakers waiting by the back door.

Peaches

Today, Rob cut down another dead peach tree. It had peaches on it, but they weren't going to be good. The tree was suffering, dying branch by branch. It finally split through the middle and collapsed.

Last year we had peaches. They were small and wormy, but wonderfully sweet and flavorful. Andrew and I enjoyed picking the best of them, but the yellow jackets got the largest share.

However, since the harvest last year, I have ignored the peach trees. I haven't pruned them, sprayed them, or done anything to help them be healthy and productive. It's not that I am unwilling, although I could easily make the excuse of lack of time. It is that I am ignorant of fruit trees. I don't know what to do with them except to let them grow. I did buy some spray and a book on pruning, but I can't make much sense of either.

My father had fruit trees. Unfortunately, I didn't pay attention as he walked out to the garden with the pruning shears in his hand or the big sprayer on his back. After I grew up, moved far away, and established my own home, I wished I could return to my parent's house for a while to consciously learn all the things that hadn't been of interest while I was growing up. I'd like to learn to make jelly, to identify birds and flowers, to fix the washer, to make things in the wood shop...and to take care of fruit trees.

But I lived far away, and adult life crowded in. So I got only a few days at a time with my parents—never long enough to learn all these things. Now it is too late, and so my peach trees die.

22

Cherries

Unlike our peaches, our cherry trees have brought us great delight this year. Last year we had only blossoms—beautiful, snowy-white blossoms—but no fruit. This year after a burst of flowering beauty, we have fruit—bright, round, tempting fruit.

Our neighbor April and Andrew and I love to pick the fruit. One night my brother Gregg and his daughters came over to pick. Andrew, age 6, had a wonderful time teaching 18–month-old Christina how to pick cherries. He praised her profusely, even when she dropped a shriveled, brown cherry into the bucket. We've had cherries for supper almost every night and have saved some in the freezer for winter. Our neighbor Carol baked us a pie with cherries we gave her, and I expect to get some cherry jam from my brother for Christmas. In all, it has been a cherry celebration!

But one question remains in my mind: "Who ever decided that cherries are good to eat?" You see, our cherries are not bing cherries, sweet and delicious to eat right from the tree. No, our cherries are pie cherries and must be cooked with sugar—lots of sugar. Raw, they are unbelievably sour. Were I foraging for food, I would try one of these cherries only once, and then pass them by as inedible. A woman of great imagination and ingenuity must have been the first to decide to pick cherries and experiment with them. I honor this ancestor of great insight, because she could imagine that something so sour could be made so delicious.

Blackberries 1

When we moved to this house, Rob was delighted to find a blackberry patch in the back corner of our property. Over the years of our marriage, I have learned that few things give Rob as much satisfaction as clearing out a bunch of brush. I have teasingly called him my "bushman."

So the blackberry patch, or more correctly blackberry bramble, became his latest challenge. Throughout our first winter Rob found time to go out to the patch, uproot weeds, cut down saplings, and trim dead vines. He got cold, scratched, scraped, and blistered; but when the berries came, he picked them with satisfaction.

Then last winter other tasks took priority, and the berry patch was left untended. This summer the weeds and the saplings are back with little evidence left that Rob ever spent any time and energy there.

Many of our tasks in life are like this blackberry patch; they never stay done. We face an unending need to launder clothes, cook meals, wash dishes, buy groceries, sweep, and mop. Yet in these daily tasks our lives take shape. Indeed, the unending jobs test our true attitudes. My mother used to say, "It's not so important that we do what we like to do. What is really important is that we like what we have to do."

Blackberries 2

Today Rob and I were talking about the blackberries. I asked if he planned to be "bushman" again this winter. He shrugged, "I've come to admire the blackberries for their wildness." Blackberries are at home in inaccessible places: they snuggle up to swamps, hide in the woods, and grow on steep slopes. We tended our blackberry patch but it remains untamed. The spines hold you at bay and resist your entering the midst of the patch. You must be content to skirt the edges. If you persist in entering, the branches close behind you, grabbing your clothes and holding you tight until you make a painful retreat. Any new growth either reaches out to claim new ground or intertwines in the bramble to make it even more impenetrable. With every year the blackberries become more independent of care and wild in nature. Yet, they produce profusely, yielding up buckets of berries.

Although blackberries seem built by God to rebuff taming and cultivation, they create their own unique place of nurturing. We have seen kittens emerge from the patch, birthed and suckled by their mother in what she saw as a place of safety. Blackberries form a fable for parents. Planted and nurtured as young, after some years the berry bushes reach out and crisscross. Rebelling against their planter's rows, they form their own pattern. Only as they begin to become their own creation do they begin to produce berries, plump and juicy, as well as become able to nurture others. Similarly, I hope Andrew will produce good deeds and be nurturing to others as he grows to be independent from us.

Mulberries

Andrew keeps asking for either a mulberry tree or a willow tree. Perhaps it's genetic, since my family had both a willow and a mulberry, and they were my favorite trees as a child. I remember sitting under the willow, with its leaf umbrella hanging all around me, and pretending it was my secret castle. I remember the mulberry tree as being full of yummy mulberries. We used to spread old sheets under the branches and shake the tree. The ripe mulberries tumbled down; and we gathered them, eating as we worked.

Andrew loves mulberries and will eat them as fast as he can pick them. He always remembers where we found them and will make a special request to return. He says they remind him of Granny, my mother, and the fun times they spent in the woods near her home. So he wants a mulberry tree of his own.

Unfortunately, you can't just buy a mulberry tree like you can a peach or plum or cherry. In fact, people ignore or scorn mulberries as if they were the low-class citizens of the fruit family. Why is that so? Mulberries are naturally sweet, not sour like cherries; are rarely buggy or wormy, like apples; don't have seeds, like blackberries; and don't need pruning and spraying to thrive, like peaches. They are delicious right off the tree. They also make wonderful jelly and syrup, and can be frozen with almost no effort. So how come they have a bad reputation? I remain baffled.

But many people also go through life unacknowledged and underappreciated, and some people have a reputation they can't live down. The mulberry challenges me to look deeper, and like Andrew, I wish we had a mulberry tree.

Flowers

Mrs. Webb had planted beautiful flowerbeds while she owned our house. As I pass by them today, I'm glad she can't see them. They are overrun with wild violets, monkey faces, and a score of unidentified weeds. It would pain her to see her flowers untended.

It is not that I don't like flowers. I am very grateful that Mrs. Webb planted so many perennials. I watch for the first crocus of spring. I love picking an armload of daffodils for Easter. I'm delighted by the trilliums and the bluebells. I'm charmed when Andrew runs in with a bouquet of iris, sweet peas, and dandelions. And I'm honored when Rob stops to cut me a single rose.

But we all must make choices in life from the many needs that surround us. We must choose how we will use our gifts of time and talent, and we must decide what things to ignore. I have chosen to spend my time cultivating plants that grow food. So the flowers must fight their own battles against weeds with no help from me.

But…I don't think this choice is forever. A time will come when I will no longer have a child to take to the park, or to challenge to Monopoly™, or to snuggle with while I read aloud. I also will not have the spontaneous hugs and declarations of, "You're the best mom in the whole world!" Then I think I will need the happy faces of flowers in the house, and, with a tinge of sorrow, I will have the time to nurture them.

Mint

A friend gave me two mint plants: one spearmint and one peppermint. I don't know which is which. I know only two things about mint: it will grow almost anywhere, and it spreads rapidly. So I planted it where nothing else (not even weeds) would grow: in a narrow space between the house and the sidewalk. It receives brutal afternoon sun and then total shade. The soil always looks dry, hard-packed, and devoid of nutrients.

Both mints have survived, but one has really thrived. It has spread to a thick patch about five feet long and wide enough to hide most of the sidewalk. Surely God made this plant to be an astonishing example of endurance in the hard places of life.

Over the past month, both mints have been blooming with pretty, feathery, purple spikes. Almost immediately, a swarm of wasps came to feed on the flowers. They are black with orange abdomens and a single yellow stripe, a wasp I have never seen before. There seem to be no other bees on the mint, and these wasps are on nothing else. In fact, taking a careful look, I realize they are only on the kind of mint that is thriving.

The wasps and the mint again make me amazed at the variety of God's creation. The mint, which will grow anywhere, is pollinated by a wasp that only this kind of mint seems to attract. The wasp appears from nowhere to feed on its host plant, the mint, and then disappears. It reminds me that every creature, including myself, has a purpose and is blessed with astonishing characteristics by God.

Cabbage and Broccoli

I took my knife and cut some second-growth cabbages this morning. They are small and compact, a bit chewed on by tiny creatures, but quite tasty. In case you don't know, each cabbage plant makes one big cabbage, which is cut early in the summer. Then, if left in the ground, some cabbage plants will grow half a dozen small cabbages around where the big one was cut. These I call "second-growth cabbages." They are a bonus after the main crop is finished. Broccoli does much the same: after the first big head of broccoli, the plant continues to grow single spears.

However, not all cabbages and broccoli continue to bear fruit. Some cabbages simply collapse and die after the head is cut. Likewise, some broccoli plants bolt and make spiky, bitter flowers instead of the compact spears that are good to eat. Why does one plant remain productive while the next one dies or turns bitter? Both receive the same sun, soil, and water. It is one of the mysteries of gardening.

Why do some people continue to make productive use of their talents after their retirement, or why do some mothers continue to find children to nurture after their own have grown? Why do others simply hole up in their homes, of little use to other people...or to themselves? This too is a mystery.

One of my fervent prayers is, "Lord, let me be a second-growth cabbage. Use me again, after my main task in life is finished."

Brussels Sprouts

Today I again looked at the Brussels sprouts I'm growing for the first time. I have no idea when they should be picked. Again, the uncertainty and the effort needed to pick them left them on the plant. I simply sighed and walked away, wondering to myself, "How did Brussels sprouts ever become a food?"

The Brussels sprout plant is quite large, larger than its cousin the broccoli, with big leaves that grow in a sort of spiral up a sturdy stalk. The Brussels sprouts grow singly, one each at the base of each leaf. They are small and insignificant. In contrast, the leaves are big and green and quite appealing, especially when covered with droplets of water.

How did my ancestors, so many centuries ago, choose the tiny Brussels sprout? Were I a gatherer looking for tonight's meal, the Brussels sprout plant would catch my attention, but I would pick the leaves. They would quickly fill my basket and make a substantial meal. I find it hard to imagine even noticing the little sprouts, far less taking the time to pick each one. I would be glad to hurry home, my task complete, even though the leaves I picked might be tough and bitter.

Could it be that I am looking at the plant too much from my modern, hurried perspective? My schedule often demands that meals appear almost instantaneously, and I frequently sacrifice flavor for simply filling. It might be that this was not the case with my ancestors. Perhaps unhurried, they sought for the most flavorful part of the plant and took time to pick and prepare it.

Spiders

When I finally cut some Brussels sprouts, I discovered I had brought in with them a large, brown, garden spider. Trying to free her by encouraging her to run out the side of the basket, I poked at her. With each poke, the spider clung even more tightly to her Brussels sprout. Only when I threatened her with drowning, did she leave her familiar setting and dash out of the basket to freedom.

As I gently prodded the spider trying to free it, I realized she perceived my attempts to help as totally threatening. Seeing the spider desperately trying to hide, I could feel her great fear of me.

When I was a child, I was irrationally fearful of spiders. I particularly feared going to the basement because spiders lived down there. I remember believing that if Mom or Dad were in the basement, then the spiders couldn't hurt me. However, the thought of going to the basement alone sent shivers through my whole body.

As a parent, I am determined not to pass my fear of spiders along to Andrew. We look for webs in the woods. We talk about how useful spiders are. And when we see a spider, we watch it. There was a beautiful, big, yellow and black spider in the garden last year, and we watched it for weeks. The result has been as I hoped: Andrew is not afraid of spiders. But the surprising result is that I am no longer afraid, either.

Squash

The squash vine borer moth flies at night in June, laying her eggs in the stem of the squash plants as the young plants poke out of the ground. Then, when the plant is big and healthy and about to produce much squash, the insects hatch into worms; and the worms eat the stem from the inside. Almost overnight the squash plant wilts and dies.

To protect our plants, I cover them with screen when they first come out of the ground. After a few weeks I uncover them and let them grow.

This summer when I took the screens off of the squash plants, they looked all crunched and bent and small. They particularly looked sad next to the two plants I never got around to covering with screen. I wondered, "Did I do the right thing? Have I stunted the squash?" But by the next week you could not see any difference between them in growth. The following week, my two uncovered plants collapsed and died, while my "stunted" ones remained healthy.

As a parent, I try to keep in mind that sometimes we need to risk stunting to enable strong growth later. Sometimes, we need to stand on our principles, even if all the other kids seem to be thriving without the same principles. We must continue to believe that kids need our restrictions and morals to protect them from potential dangers and temptations. The restrictions will not delay the child's maturity for long and may help them be old enough and responsible enough to turn down choices that can lead to heartbreak and even death.

Bugs

Mosquitoes, caterpillars, and slugs are all a part of gardening, particularly if you are a mediocre gardener and believe gardens are best shared with God's smallest creatures. We do make an attempt to encourage the bugs to go elsewhere. We plant lots of marigolds and nasturtiums, and Andrew and I concoct a pungent natural bug spray. We spend a wonderful afternoon stirring up this bug brew from soap and water, garlic and onions, horseradish and hot pepper, and anything else we want to throw in. It works pretty well, provided it doesn't just sit in my refrigerator.

But mostly we cheer for nature's natural predators. Last year Andrew came running in shouting in alarm, "Mom, April found a praying mantis, and she's got it in a jar! She says she's going to keep it!" I went out, and after we all spent time watching it, Andrew and I persuaded April to let it go...in our garden. I've been told if you took away all the insect eaters, like praying mantises, spiders, birds, and bats, the earth would be defoliated in a matter of a few weeks. We enjoy the spiderwebs in the garden, and the birds as they swoop in the evening. So we don't spray, for spraying would kill the spiders and the praying mantises and the ladybugs and the honeybees.

Another reason for not spraying is that even the "bad" bugs make the garden more interesting. It's fun to run after the cabbage butterflies, or be surprised by a grasshopper, or find a giant tobacco worm, or even watch a group of stinkbugs pile up on each other. All of this interest is worth a few bites out of the vegetables.

Compost

As long as Rob and I have had gardens, we have had compost piles. In Brooklyn our compost pile was actually bigger than our garden. Something in me can't throw away carrot peels and apple cores. However, as I am a mediocre gardener, I am also a mediocre composter. I don't turn it regularly, or pile it in any container or in any systematic manner. I simply make a pile and expect nature to take its own course. Some years my compost pile has resembled a haystack. When left undisturbed through the winter, the matted grass on the top prevented the contents from decomposing. But even in my most untended piles, the dark rich compost develops at the bottom of the pile.

Today, as I sent Andrew out to empty my bucket of kitchen leavings on the compost pile, I considered how, when I was Andrew's age, I didn't even know the word *compost*. Compost gives me hope for our world's future. When I think our economic, social, and justice issues are insurmountable, I am reminded that we are doing better in the area of caring for the environment. Over the years more and more individuals have decided to recycle, conserve, and protect, and so as a society, we have made progress. We do have cleaner air and water, and plants and animals are being protected better. Andrew is a good example of the kids his age: he can't pass an aluminum can without picking it up; he always looks for fish line on the beach; he insists we turn off the water when we brush our teeth; and he happily runs out to empty the compost bucket.

Parsley

This year when our peppers came from the Hunger Coalition, along came an assortment of herbs. I gave most of them to Jerie, planted a few, and thought I would plant the rest later. Somehow the time to plant them never came. They just sat in the yard in their little two-inch cubes. Slowly, different ones began to die: first the dill, then the basil. Finally, only the parsley was left.

By this time weeks had passed since these herbs had first made their appearance in our yard. I passed the pots of parsley every time I went to the garden or out to the compost pile. Its tenacity began to tug at me. Finally, Andrew and I took spades one afternoon and planted the parsley in the untended flower box in front of the house.

Over the summer the parsley has stayed there. It has not grown, but it has not died either. I passed it today and was struck again by its endurance. It reminds me of the various neglected plants that live on my kitchen windowsill. Starved for the attention of regular water and plant food, they don't flourish; but they don't die either. I have a little marigold Andrew planted in school. It grew a single, spindly stem with a few leaves, and not too long ago it bloomed. It had one tiny flower about a half inch in diameter, but nonetheless it was a marigold.

It seems that built right into life is the determination to keep living, to hold on no matter what the conditions are. It makes me believe God must care very much for life, to have given to every living thing such a strong will to continue living.

Late September

I just came in from the garden and need to rest. I should have gone out and picked yesterday, but other things pushed into the forefront. That is the way it is with a garden in September. The garden is now old and scraggly, and school and work crowd out its place in our lives.

In September, the garden feels like a chore, and it is depressing to be out there. The tomatoes now ripen to an orange color and often are twisted or spoiled. Frequently, when you reach for a ripe one, your hand comes away empty as you feel the big rotten spot underneath. Only a few are the bright, red, round tomatoes of August. Oh, there is one exception: the cherry tomatoes are still round, red, unblemished, and plentiful.

But mostly the garden is a place of death. Gone are the squash, beans, radishes, lettuce, broccoli, cabbage, and onions. Even the crabgrass has turned brown. Only the peppers remain bright and green and flowering.

Ironically, the weather is perfect for gardening: cool and bright, not blistering. It is very like the weather in the spring when we planted and would come in from the garden tired, but happy and expectant. Now I am tired, but sad and contemplative, as I see the close of the season draw near.

Green Tomatoes

Tomorrow is "Clean-up Day." We've invited some of our friends to come over and help us clean up the garden and bring it to a close for the season. We will pull up, chop down, and put away. All that will remain to do after tomorrow is to spread leaves on the garden as we rake them.

As we pull up the tomato plants and unwind them from their cages, we will pick all the remaining green tomatoes. These we pack loosely in boxes, making three layers of tomatoes, each separated by newspapers. The boxes will then be covered completely and carried to the basement to await a miracle.

I say it is a miracle because if you pick a green tomato and set it in the sun it will usually shrivel and rot. But packed away in complete darkness, each tomato will ripen in its own time. They will not ripen as red and sweet as August tomatoes straight from the garden, but they will be good nonetheless. Each week when I go down to check through the layers, I find it rather awesome to discover the red, ripe tomatoes waiting there. And when Andrew and I arrive at the food pantry with our laundry basket of tomatoes, we revel in the exclamations of, "You still have tomatoes!?!"

The past two seasons, we have had the very last of the tomatoes for Thanksgiving Dinner. I hope that will work out again this year. It seems a fitting close to our Hunger Garden to serve its fruits as we say, "Thank you, God, for all your blessings."

second season

Eagerness

The air has a touch of spring this morning, so I went out to the garden—just for a peek. It is really still winter, but a hint of change in the temperature brings a stirring I can feel deep in my soul. Mom used to take us children to Beaver Dam State Park to tramp in the woods. I remember best the times when Mom would help us discover the earliest signs of spring. We found moss turning green, buds beginning to open, and little sprouts hiding under the leaves. We sensed we were seeing the beginning of something exciting, and winter didn't seem quite the same afterward.

Today, among the stubble of last year's garden, we found small pieces of green poking through. I know that each is a weed I will later wish to pull out or till under, but for now they are a welcome sight. They show the eagerness of the ground. I am eager, too—eager to plant and have things grow, eager to share and have great bounty to give away, eager to renew friendships that have grown along with the garden, eager to feel the dirt in my hands and know my part of God's creation.

My mother always said she liked to go to the grocery because a full refrigerator made her feel rich and blessed. I agree, but a full garden makes me feel even richer. Our minister puts it another way. He says: "Seek to find the things which fill your heart." I count myself very fortunate to have so many things that fill my heart: my husband and son, my friends, my work, the breadth of my experiences, the closeness of God...and our garden. Today, my walk to the garden to see the spring thaw filled my heart.

Yankee Garden

When we plan our garden each year, we try to pick plants that are easy to grow, easy to harvest, and commonplace. We try to grow vegetables we think people will want and will know how to use and cook. Not until this spring did I realize the cultural statement our garden and its choice of plants makes. Our garden is a Yankee garden. A neighbor has an equally large garden, but except for tomatoes he does not repeat a single item in our garden.

We have: green beans; lettuce and spinach; summer and winter squash; bell and sweet banana peppers; broccoli and cabbages; cucumbers and radishes…and tomatoes.

He has: black-eyed peas; collard and mustard greens; several kinds of corn; chili and hot peppers; turnips and kale; okra…and tomatoes.

His garden might be called a "soul food garden," but whatever the name, it certainly represents a different culture than our garden.

Coming to know his garden, I am again reminded of how blind we are to our own cultural attitudes and assumptions. We do not grow food that "everyone knows how to cook." In fact, we grow food that "I and my culture know how to cook." In light of all the different cultures in our country, not to mention the world, I am humbled that I missed so basic an understanding. Perhaps next year we'll grow turnips or okra.

State Fair Veggies

We have a little tradition out in the garden when we pick a particularly large, ripe, and unblemished vegetable, no matter whether it is a radish, a tomato, or a head of broccoli. We hold it up for everyone to see and announce, "I found a State Fair Veggie." We all "ooh" and "ah" before it is put into the bag. With few exceptions, we take these "best of the crop" to the food pantry. The unblemished vegetables last longest without refrigeration and are the most appealing to people accustomed to grocery produce. We can salvage for ourselves those vegetables with flaws because we can put them directly into our refrigerator.

At a deeper level, we find a special joy to be able to give our very best. As in the Bible when people brought the best of their flock to be sacrificed at the temple, so we bring the best of the garden to this work of feeding the poor, a work we believe is God's work.

One very human need is that of presenting our best to God. Some people would say we each need to find our calling or find God's plan for our lives. But for me, it is easier to understand the notion of bringing my best. That means choosing jobs that match our beliefs. That means allotting the best of our time and energy to being parents. Our calling should not be shunted to the edges of our hours when our day is spent. I am grateful Rob has been able to work to help the homeless. Likewise, I am grateful we have put mothering at the center of my life. For us, that creates harmony between our beliefs and our efforts. It is a way to live out God's blessings.

Lettuce

This year we planted an early garden of radishes, lettuce, and spinach. It was so wonderful to go out on a crisp morning and see the little dots of green sprinkling the dark ground as the lettuce sprouted. What fun we have had picking and using the lettuce leaves. The fun is partly because it is the first harvest, but partly because we have such a great variety—green leaf, red leaf, oak leaf, bib, romaine, and iceberg, along with a few varieties I don't have names for. When I send Andrew and April out to the garden to pick some lettuce, they return with what can best be described as a bouquet of lettuce.

The older I get the more creation moves me, not for its immense size or fantastic spectacles, but for its plethora of kinds. I have come to believe that variety is one of the main tenets of God's work. How amazing that God makes every person, snowflake, and grain of sand different from every other person, snowflake, and grain of sand. This sense of amazement helps me when I wish to make God small and limited. I think when we want all people to be alike, act alike, or follow the same beliefs and culture, we are being the most unlike God. If we believe God has created each person to be unique and if we believe God has been active in people's lives throughout history, then we must conclude God has had a hand in the many different cultures and peoples of the world, and God approves of them.

I have come to believe this strongly with regard to religions. Like our many varieties of lettuce, I believe we should celebrate and cherish and wonder at the bouquet of religious thought God has given to this world.

Beans 1

We planted a long row of beans today. A garden doesn't seem complete without them. The seeds are easy to hold and fun for little fingers to plant. It's amusing to see beans sprout because they back themselves out of the ground stem first. They are also good for the soil, enriching it with nitrogen. I always watch eagerly for the first beans and make the first picking when they are young, tender, and flavorful. Lightly steamed, they taste delicious.

But I know the plants will begin to produce a lot of beans in the hot days of July. Picking beans then becomes a sweaty, prickly, backbreaking task. The green beans hide in the leaves, and the plants intertwine, making them difficult to untangle. The kettle fills too slowly. Rob particularly hates to pick beans. If there is a personalized hell for each of us, Rob's might be picking beans all day, every day, in July.

On reflection, beans represent the hard work of a garden. In the spring the weather is pleasant, the soil is loose and bare, and we share great anticipation in planting. But by midsummer, the plants have crowded together, the harvest is coming on fast, and the sun beats down on your head and back. The labor is hard, hot, and relentless, but must be done or the crop will spoil, and the hope of the spring will prove senseless.

I think many of life's most important tasks, whether parenting or employment, are like the beans. No matter how much you love your job or your children, or how committed you are to your career, at times it is just plain hard work. But without that work, the harvest is lost.

Beans 2

This year we let the best bean picking days go by. We knew they were ready, but none of us could face the task. It was hot and other vegetables that were easier to harvest were ripening quickly as well. So the beans stayed on the vine.

Today Jerie and I decided to simply pull up the plants and pick the rest of the beans off. Having piled the plants in the shade, we sat quietly talking as we turned the plants upside down and snapped off the beans. Commenting on the giant, overgrown beans, we got to talking about our grandparents. My grandmother used to say that a long, fat, mature bean had "real nourishment." She would cook these big, tough beans with bacon or a ham hock for hours, until they were almost brown in color. Jerie remembered her grandfather taking her out to see his Kentucky Wonder pole beans. Some of them were nearly a foot long. How proud he was of the big ones!

We talked about how ideas of nutrition have changed. We now eat raw many vegetables that past generations always cooked. We agreed that we preferred slim, young, tender beans to the long, fat, tough beans of our grandparents.

I got to wondering which beans are now picked for the blue ribbons at the state fair. Do the judges choose the small, crisp early beans, or do they reward the giant, knobby, mature beans? I think I'll look next time the fair is in town.

Showers

After a morning out in the garden, particularly when it's hot, I am especially grateful for a long cool shower. Over the years, my morning shower has become my sacred time, my prayer time. There is something very redemptive about a shower.

First, the water pours over you, washing away not only the dirt, sweat, sunscreen, and garden prickles, but also the cares of yesterday. It leaves me fresh to face the new day.

Second, it is a time when I can present myself most easily as I am, without pretense. I find myself most able to be truthful about my shortcomings and my need for guidance.

Third, the water has come to be a sign of blessing for me. After I've bathed and shampooed, I like to simply stand with the water streaming down my back. It is then I am most grateful for all that I have and all that I have experienced.

Last, standing in the quiet, with the morning light pouring through the window and the water pouring over me, I am my most receptive to God's spirit.

However, not every shower is a time of prayer. Some days the place of peace I try to clear in my mind immediately fills with the cares of the day, or generalized anxiety, or an inane popular song. But other days—particularly days when I have been out among the plants and soil—my mind fills with a hymn of praise, a need of others, or a solution to a problem. Then I feel the touch of God on my life, and I am assured of God's guidance.

Morning Light

My grandmother grew up when electricity was not common on farms. She used to turn on the lights only when necessary. In particular, she did not turn them on when she got up in the morning. I remember finding Grandma puttering around making breakfast in the semi-darkness. She said it helped her start the day quietly and calmly let the day brighten naturally. Turning on the lights inside, she felt, shut her off from awareness of things outside.

It's hard for me not to switch on the light the very first thing after stumbling downstairs. I'm in a hurry to make breakfast and fill the lunch box. But when it is my turn for the shower, I flip off the light just before I step into the water. A window in the shower lets me really enjoy the morning light there. Sometimes it comes in bright golden streams, changing to colors as it passes through the stained-glass panel hanging in the window. Then the water drops sparkle like thousands of crystals. Sometimes the light sneaks in with a quiet silvery glow that brings calmness to my soul. A few times it is still dark, and the shower stall becomes a place of mystery. My eyes slowly adjust, searching out the growing light.

When I am an old lady without any rush, I plan to adopt my grandmother's habit. I will let the light emerge, bringing peace to my whole morning. But maybe the time when I need peace is now. Tomorrow, I think I'll pack Andrew's lunch by the natural light of morning. Maybe it will help me comprehend that each day is God's new creation.

Zucchini

Zucchini and all its summer squash sisters rank as the most amazing of our garden plants. A little more than a month after we plant the seeds in the ground, the plants are five feet across with leaves as big as small pizzas. I saw a leaf today that was easily sixteen to eighteen inches in diameter. When the fruits come on, they grow at an even faster rate. Though we try to check the garden at least every two or three days, I am often amazed to find zucchinis more than a foot long. I think, "Did I miss this one when I picked before? Has it really grown so big in such a short period of time?" The biggest zucchini I ever saw was about three feet long and so heavy I could barely lift it. I cooked it in a Native American stew and served almost thirty people.

But equally as impressive as its miracle of growth is the zucchini's tenacious determination to live in spite of adversity and disability. Although we carefully screen the young squash plants to protect them from the squash bore, we still have that pest. The eggs of the moth are laid in the squash sprout. The larvae hatch in the stem and proceed to eat and destroy the stem at the base of the plant. Some of the zucchini plants wilt and die almost immediately, but most continue to produce and flourish. Sometimes the stem is so riddled with holes that it seems to be holding on by only a thread. How do they manage to stay healthy when their base—their connection to the ground and their source of water—is so totally compromised? I don't know, but they have my admiration. If I am ever struck with a disability, I hope I, too, may keep producing fruit.

Broccoli

When we planted our broccoli plants in early May, we conducted an experiment: we interspersed them with the green peppers, thinking the broccoli would produce early and the peppers late. We could cut the broccoli down around the time the peppers were coming on strong. For weeks our broccoli plants grew bigger and bigger but showed no sign of budding. Of course, what we eat is the bud of the flower. Finally, we gave up on the broccoli and even considered cutting it down. Then last week, the third week in July, we suddenly realized we had broccoli heads forming on every plant. The heads were the big 10" kind. They turned out to be among our finest vegetables.

I like the idea of late blooming. It is extra sweet to accomplish something later in life than expected. Every high school class has someone who returns for the twentieth reunion looking unexpectedly fashionable, poised, and accomplished. I get great pleasure out of playing catch with my son, partly because I learned to play baseball and owned my first mitt as an adult. I also learned to drive a car in my thirties, not my teens, and I started to write in my forties.

The idea of late blooming is the promise of hope:

- hope that love can be found after the death of a spouse
- hope that a new career is possible when a job sours
- hope that it is never too late to follow a dream

I'm glad our broccoli was a late bloomer.

White Butterflies

From late May to late September, common cabbage butterflies create a white, flitting presence in our garden. They zip and circle, land briefly, then flutter on again. Unfortunately, white butterflies mean cabbage worms. To fight the worms, we catch the butterflies. In fact, we pay Andrew and his friends ten cents a butterfly. The children take their nets and run and run until they've caught themselves a dollar's worth, for which they get a ten-cent bonus. By that time they are pretty well exhausted. The butterflies have a distinct advantage. They can fly wherever they choose, while people must travel through the rows and be sure not to step on the plants. The task requires quickness, balance, cunning, and stamina. Few adults could get the ten-cent bonus.

One of the wonders of being a child is feeling rich with just one dollar. Unfortunately, one of the hard lessons of childhood is having *one* dollar and finding what you want costs *ten* dollars. We all know that feeling. Recently, we decided that Rob must have a new suit. We budgeted what we thought was adequate, only to find it was merely half the needed amount.

Dealing with money is one of my greatest challenges, and dealing with my child's wants is one of the most difficult aspects of parenting. I want Andrew to learn to work and earn money, but I don't want him caught up in the things money can buy. I want him to be content with all that he has and to have only a short Santa's list. I've concluded that to foster that in Andrew, I, too, must have a short Santa's list, and count all that I have as gifts from God.

Cabbages 1

Today I bought an insecticide and sprinkled it on my cabbages. I hate to use chemicals, but we were in danger of losing the whole crop to the cabbage worms. Other years we managed with a hot red pepper concoction. But this year the worms have not been deterred, so I turned to poison. I took three small cabbages to our pantry last week and brought one back home today. Even though it is was free for the taking, nobody wanted it because it had worm holes. I cut it up and didn't find any worms. The taste was unharmed. Standards for things have surely changed. Before refrigeration, cabbage was a mainstay of many cultures. It keeps well in root cellars and is loaded with needed vitamins. Those days were before insecticides, but not before cabbage worms. Our grandmothers simply cut away the worm holes and used the rest. But today a worm hole is considered unacceptable.

Research shows that our society has raised the standards for many aspects of life. Time spent doing laundry is as great today as before washing machines, since clothes worn once are now considered dirty. Microwave ovens have resulted in cooking a different menu for each meal, rather than cooking a big pot for the week. Computers have made penned corrections unacceptable. Greater incomes mean that more and more possessions are deemed necessary. Greater knowledge of disease or crime has spread fear of human contact.

Perhaps it is time to question our standards of material perfection—to ask if these new standards add to the quality of our spirits.

Cabbages 2

Today I was hunting around in the refrigerator to find any hidden leftovers. I pulled out a blue bag, with no idea what it contained. Out fell a cabbage that had been cut in half and stored to be used again. Instead, it had been forgotten. Seeing the black slime on the outside of the head, I gingerly removed it from the bag, and ran water over it to rinse away the rotten parts. Taking my knife I cut away the outside leaves to reveal the inside that was still good. Turning to the flat side that had been cut off, I found a little round lump of good cabbage in the center.

At first I thought, "What a strange way for me to have cut this, to trim it flat except for a round lump." I cut off the lump and proceeded to cut the cabbage into pieces to stir-fry. When I came to the lump I sliced it through the middle and was surprised to see it was a perfect, miniature cabbage. Suddenly, I realized that this cabbage had grown a new little head while it waited, forgotten in the cold and dark!

Into everyone's life come times of grief. These are times when we can feel cut to the core, only half there, lonely, and living in a cold, dark place. I do not believe that God intends for us to suffer or that God gives us suffering as a test, or that suffering is in anyway noble or righteous. I do believe that somehow, in some unfathomable way, that grief can result in new growth. We can grow to know ourselves better and renew our relationships, to find new purpose and deepen our gratitude; and we can discover that even in the cold, dark depths when we feel alone and forgotten, God has not abandoned us.

Cucumbers 1

Every year one crop seems to be "Crop of the Year." Last year, it was red hot chili peppers. We had more than we could pick, while everything else in the garden suffered from too much rain. This year the "Crown Prince of Crops" is the cucumber. Two weeks ago, when Andrew and I arrived at the food pantry, their produce table was already piled high with cucumbers. They certainly didn't need my sack full!

I asked Carolyn at the food pantry if she wanted me to take my cucumbers and the extra box to the local soup kitchen, which serves 200 people daily. She agreed, and just as I was leaving, an elderly gentleman came in with two more big bags of cucumbers. He said, "I've been gardening for forty years, and I've never had a crop of cucumbers like this before." I nodded and asked if he minded if we took his "cukes" along to the soup kitchen. He said, "Certainly, I just want somebody to use them." Off we sped to The Breadline with our multitude of cucumbers. When we walked in, the staff laughed because at that very moment they had the food slicer going, slicing cucumbers.

I try to remember the Crop of the Year when Andrew comes to me with a long list of things he can't do as well as someone else. It is hard to accept that most of the time we are all pretty ordinary. But I believe at some time each of us has the chance to excel at something. As with the old man's cucumbers, it may take years or a lifetime, but we all in our own way get to shine like the Crop of the Year.

Today was Andrew's turn to shine: he passed his swimming test.

Cucumbers 2

This afternoon Andrew and I took our wagon loaded with ripe tomatoes and walked around the neighborhood giving them away. I had done this as a child. We headed south toward the houses of the economically poor. Drawn shades and warning signs on the doors make some houses look unwelcoming and unoccupied. Usually elderly people live there, people whose experiences have made them old, tired, and wary. They answer the doorbell with suspicion and a gruff word. At first, they refused our produce. When we insisted that the tomatoes were *free* of charge, they all seemed happy to have some. One lady, who was painfully twisted with arthritis, broke into a big smile and asked for a whole bag. She said, "Now, I will put up some sauce for the winter!"

On the way home with an empty wagon, I found myself thinking about our cucumbers. This morning the cucumber vines looked old and tired, not surprising after their great yield. Thinking there would only be a few "cukes" to pick, I left my knife and gloves lying on the trash can lid. As the plants scratched my hands unmercifully, I steadily found big juicy cucumbers hiding under the leaves, hugging close to the ground; and I soon found myself in the middle of the patch, weighted down with a bag filled to the top.

How like our cucumbers our elderly neighbors seem. At first, they show prickles of fear and loneliness with no possibility for yielding fruits of friendship. But today we found hidden smiles with our tomatoes. How I wish I could find other ways to make connections with them. If I could, there might be unimagined fruits of friendship waiting there.

Neighbors

I always jump when the front door bell rings, particularly when I'm alone. My reaction to a knock at the back door is the complete opposite. Our back door represents an important part of my life: my neighbors. For some unknown reason, our neighbors come to the back door. Often the knock is that of a child, asking, "Can Andrew play?" "Can I have a drink?" "Can you come help? Victoria fell." Other times it is an adult, saying, "Do you have a cup of milk?" "Could you watch April for a few minutes?" "Would you bandage me? I just cut my finger." I learned many years ago that neighbors are one of God's greatest gifts to us.

"Policeman Dan" is one of the best of those gifts to our family. He lives two houses up and is very skilled at being a good neighbor. He knows being a good neighbor includes both borrowing and giving, both offering help and asking for help. The garden has been part of our friendship with Dan. He borrows our grass catcher and then empties it on our garden. He shares his raspberries, and we share our blackberries. We give him cherries, and he gives us his cherry jelly.

Yesterday, he said he was thinking about making some bread-'n'-butter pickles, so today I picked two big bags of cucumbers and told him to choose as many as he wanted. He was delighted, and so was I because it's always fun to share bounty. Many times when we share with him, it becomes a wonderful trade. He gets homegrown vegetables without the hot sun, and we get homemade goodies without the hot kitchen.

Truly, my life would be poorer without my neighbors.

Broken Lock

Today we discovered our garden shed was missing its lock. A little later we found the lock sawed off and cast away in the grass. We looked over the contents of the shed but could find nothing missing. Probably the would-be thieves were looking for bicycles, which are easy to sell. Fortunately there must not be a market for lawn mowers. We've been burglarized and robbed before. One of the biggest shocks came this May when Andrew's new bike was stolen from the garage only one day after we gave it to him as a present.

Being robbed always brings me up short to take a good look at myself. I try to put possessions well down the list of my priorities. We choose to live on an income the government labels as "low." We try to teach Andrew that *things* are not important. But when I am robbed, the anger and the sorrow I feel reveal to me my deep materialism. I see how much of my life I have bound up in my things. Things hold many life stories, memories, and personal histories. When my jewelry was stolen, the thief took with him many reminders of my parents, my grandparents, my friends, and places traveled. The check from the insurance company could not replace those losses.

So being robbed has taught me that I must take care not to keep my memories in my things. Although I recall my father whenever I sit down at his desk, the desk is not he; and I do not need the desk to recall him. I can think of my father wherever I am and no matter what I own. Perhaps that is partly what Jesus meant when he spoke of storing up "treasure in heaven" (Lk. 18:22).

Apples

We have an old apple tree in the backyard that the kids call the "rotten apple tree." It bears what my father used to call "early harvest" apples. I simply call them "sour apples." They are small and green and full of various-sized worm holes. But the kids love them. From midsummer till fall, the kids don't come into the kitchen for a snack. Instead, they troop out to the apple tree, scramble up in it, and pick themselves an apple.

Two days ago, Andrew and his friend Chris asked if they might pick a few of the apples. I said, "Sure," and handed them a bag. A while later, they returned to proudly present me with a peck of apples. I was tempted to sneak them out to the compost pile after Andrew went to bed. Instead, I borrowed a food mill to make applesauce. This afternoon Andrew and I set to work. We cut, cored, cooked, and then pounded them through the food mill. Andrew and I decided a food mill is a good way to build up your biceps. After an hour and a half, we had about a pint of applesauce...plus a full afternoon of companionship.

Our ancestors spent day after day canning, freezing, or preserving food. I remember my own mother in the blazing heat of the kitchen as apples were boiled, beans blanched, or tomatoes stewed. I am again grateful for all those who bring my food prepared and waiting in my cool grocery. Those people allow me to spend my summer hours doing things like going to the beach with Andrew.

Tonight we had the applesauce for supper. It was smooth and good, yes, very good—but then, so is applesauce in a forty-nine–cent jar from the grocery.

Cherries

In the first season, as I considered the extreme sourness of red pie cherries, I posed the question of how they ever became a coveted food. This year, I think we have discovered the answer to that question. This year, the cherries were sparse. Nevertheless, we looked forward to picking the bright red, juicy fruits. When picking came, few cherries made their way into our buckets! Why? Because they were sweet—sweet enough to eat right off the tree, and eat them we did. It was the same tree, but the cherries were certainly not the same. Maybe it was the weather, but more likely it was the result of fewer fruits. The tree was able to invest more sweetness in each cherry.

This is the principle behind thinning: removing some fruit from the tree so that the remaining fruit will grow bigger and sweeter. As a mediocre gardener, I find it difficult to pluck early fruit, prune roses, sucker tomatoes, or thin lettuce. I know expert gardeners cut and prune plants with seeming ease, but I am torn between thinking I'll hurt the plant and having an odd sense of the unfairness of cutting back the plant's effort to produce.

I find it true in my life too. I am reluctant to throw out clutter, to turn down requests, and to trim back my pursuits. My house is filled with possessions, and my life is filled with activities. In the seeming abundance of my life, I wonder if the sweetness of each item or interest is diminished. Cutting back on all parts of our lives might add unexpected sweetness to what we do. It certainly improves the taste of cherries when the tree grows fewer fruits.

Gardener's Hands

Yesterday, Andrew and I went to the old Illinois state capitol. The tour guides reenacted conversations that might have taken place there 150 years ago. It was all fun and humorous and very distant from my current life in Springfield. Often when I hear or read about history, I wonder how the women of the past managed. How did they care for so many children and yet accomplish so many household tasks? How were they happy on the frontier, isolated from everyone but their own family? How did they keep their sanity during the long winters, with so many energetic children in such small cabins and no TV? I shake my head in puzzlement.

But today, as I came in from the garden and stepped into the shower, I noticed my hands. They are gardener's hands: deep-tanned and rough, with dirt under the fingernails. They are hands like I remember seeing my mother have, hands like my grandmother had, and hands like women of the ages past. I suddenly felt connected to all those women who have come in from the garden over the generations.

A few minutes later, I had scrubbed the nails clean and smoothed the roughness with skin cream. My gardener's hands have disappeared for the moment, but the feeling of connection remains. That is a feeling I hope to keep forever.

Rain

It has been raining all day—a gardener's rain: just a steady, gentle patter. The air feels cooled, washed clean. I looked at my calendar and rejoiced to see a totally blank space under today's date. So like the rain, I feel unhurried. Steady, gentle activity has left me calmed and smiling. Summer rain can be so magical, such a blessing. I always wonder at people's description of a quiet, drizzly, silvery day as being dark and gloomy and something to moan about.

As a gardener in rural, southern Illinois, my father always identified with the farmers. Whenever he watered his garden, he would shake his head grimly knowing that thousands of acres of corn and beans didn't have the luxury of water from a hose. I vividly recall my father getting very annoyed at the St. Louis TV weatherman who announced cheerfully, "It will be another beautiful weekend. There is no break in sight for the terrific summer weather we have enjoyed these past few weeks. So be sure and go to the parks and swimming pools and have fun!"

My father's response was, "Doesn't that fella know how desperately we need rain? The most beautiful summer weather we could have right now would be a few days of steady rain!"

We've gone quite a long time without rain, and the ground has been thirsty. Today the water is steadily quenching that thirst. The rain seems like God is gladdening the ground, and my spirit has been gladdened too. In addition, the rain brought my father close in my memory.

Weed Chopping

The one job in the garden Andrew always wants to do is "weed chopping." I don't mean pulling weeds up by the roots. I mean savagely attacking the plants and chopping them to bits. When the broccoli or lettuce bolt and become too bitter to eat, Andrew can be counted on to make the leaves fly in all directions. Any place weeds grow tall—in the yard, garden, or alley—Andrew finds great relish in their destruction.

Andrew has become quite a collector and connoisseur of weed choppers. He uses all sorts of sticks and pieces of metal. Among them are a car antenna and a broken cue stick. A confirmed scavenger, Andrew keeps us entertained and cluttered with what he finds, and a frequent identification is: "This will make a good weed chopper!"

What interests me most is the ferocity with which he goes about the task. Some might say, "He is reacting to the pervasive violence in our society." Others might say, "He is just being a boy." I think it goes deeper. It is a reaction to being a child, to feeling powerless, to feeling surrounded by bigger, stronger, guiding adults. These feelings may be natural for any child who grows up with parents who care enough to supervise and instruct. When Andrew chops a plant, I think he is venting frustration basic to growing up. Hopefully, this need will lessen as he gains more of a sense of self-control and independence. As I watch him, I am reminded that being a child is not an easy task.

By the way, Andrew disagrees with my analysis. He says, "It's just plain fun."

Nightshade

Today Jerie and I decided to pull up as much nightshade as we could. The time for weeding has passed, and we have left the garden to the crabgrass and other weeds. But we decided to pull up the nightshade because it is going to seed. We think maybe if we pull up the plants before the seeds are mature, we might not have quite so many nightshades next year. Rob said, "I think it is a futile effort," and went off to mow, something *I* think is a futile effort!

My decision to pull up the nightshade really is deeper than wishful weed control. I want to pull it up because those little berries, round and black and luscious-looking, are deadly. It makes me uneasy to have them growing in the garden. I know their close relatives—the tomato, potato, and green pepper—also have poisonous parts, but the fruits are nourishing and delicious. I know that I won't eat any of those little black berries, and I've taught the children to leave them alone. Throughout the summer I have given the nightshade no more attention than any other weed. But come September, and the appearance of those little black fruits, the nightshade causes a particular shudder of abhorrence, and I wish to be rid of it.

I hope that some of my bad habits will be like the nightshade. Even though I may have gone long years excusing and ignoring my procrastination, messiness, laziness, disorganization, anger, and so on, I hope someday I will look at each of these and say, "This has no place in my life!" I wish to say it with such vehemence, it will compel me to pull it up and cast it away.

Morning Glories

In Illinois, the worst weed for gardeners is the common morning glory. Its seeds were laid down in the prairie centuries ago, and it evolved to thrive in that prairie (and in my garden). Its deep roots allow it to escape the prairie fire (and my tiller). Its runners can travel far below the matted grasses (or my black plastic) before finding a hole and pushing to the top. And, it grows as a vine, reaching the sun by growing up the prairie grass (or my pepper plants).

My father nicknamed the morning glory "strangleweed." He fought the menace year after year. It shades, crowds, and strangles the plants you've planted. When you pull it up, it holds so tightly to the other plants you can uproot or damage the very plant you were trying to protect. But not everyone scorns this plant. Jerie's neighbor allows the morning glories to grow over his tomatoes. He says, "It helps strengthen the tomatoes and hold them up off the ground." And a house nearby has a whole bank covered with common morning glories.

When I was a child, our neighbor planted blue morning glories around the telephone pole. It really galled my father that anyone would intentionally plant a close relative of strangleweed. But I loved those big blue flowers. They had a white star surrounded by velvety tissue of deep indigo. I thought they looked like fairy skirts as I twirled a blossom in my fingers. Today, Andrew stopped at the abandoned house on the corner to pick me a morning glory. The color was the same deep blue, and as I twirled it in my fingers, I smiled and said, "Thank you."

Goldenrod

Across the alley from our garden stands a tall goldenrod plant in beautiful bloom. The goldenrod has grown undisturbed all summer, and I am quite fearful its full glory will attract attention. Of course, the purpose of the bright flowers is to attract attention, but of the bees and other pollinating insects, not of someone who might chop it down. Early this week, I was talking to Policeman Dan. I made a point of saying how beautiful the goldenrod was. "What! That old weed!?!" he laughed. "Yes," I said, "We had bouquets of goldenrod at our wedding. I want to collect the seed after it's through blooming and plant them around the end of the blackberry patch." He shook his head and walked off, but he hasn't chopped it down.

Goldenrod is a good lesson in what a bad reputation can do to you. It blooms during hay fever season and is laden with pollen, so naturally it was thought to stimulate people's allergies. We now know that goldenrod pollen is too heavy to be carried in the air and breathed in. The real culprit of hay fever is ragweed. Ragweed blooms at the same time as goldenrod, but its "flower" is green and easily overlooked. It has no need of bright colors to call attention to itself because ragweed is pollinated by wind, not insects. Being very lightweight, ragweed pollen is borne everywhere in the air and is highly irritating to breathe.

Unfortunately, although we now know the goldenrod is innocent, the reputation remains, so this stately flower with the delicate yellow blossoms remains a "bad weed."

Houston 1

Houston, our cat, is dying. Except for fish, all people and pets in my life have done their dying distant from me in distant hospitals, distant towns, or the back room of a veterinarian clinic. Perhaps the most poignant example was my mother. She got on the train in Idaho and never arrived home in Ohio. She died in Chicago surrounded by strangers. To me, dying has not been a process but rather a sudden disappearance from my life.

Houston's dying is a strange but generous gift. Never a cat who tolerated being held, now she wants to be cuddled and stroked. Yesterday, I was sick and spent the day lying in bed holding her. It made me recall the times I held Andrew as a baby, rocking him by the hour on our porch swing. When he was three, he caught the stomach flu, and I got to sit and hold him all day long. I recall memories of Houston mothering her kittens. The day the kittens were born, she did not go off and hide. She crawled onto Andrew's bed, woke me up, and gave birth to the kittens with us watching. If I would start to leave the room, she would come after me meowing pleadingly, as if to say, "Don't leave me alone with these babies!" Later she calmed down and was a wonderful mother.

So now Houston is dying. It is a quiet ending, a time to hold her and know she wishes me to be near, to recall her life with appreciation and find its closing. My last gift from Houston, the cat who shared birth with me, is to have her share death with me as well. It has made me less fearful of the end of life for myself and for those I love.

Houston 2

I awoke this morning to find a surprise: Houston is lying on our bed. This seems incomprehensible to me, because today is Friday. Houston is dying and has neither eaten nor drunk since last Saturday. We thought last Tuesday she might not make it through the night. Today is Friday, three days later.

Last night after we went to bed, Rob and I were holding her and stroking her; but before I fell asleep, I took her back down to the box of rags in the closet where she has spent much of her last days. I thought that would be her wish. But sometime during the night, she got up, walked the length of the house, up a flight of stairs, and somehow managed to jump up on the bed. How did she do it?

I can only stand in awe at the strong grip life has on life. Living creatures hold on to a mighty will to live. We often speak of the fragility of existence, but Houston has made me see that life is not fleeting and fragile, but tenacious. The soul is not yielded up lightly or on a whim.

I can only conclude that God must deeply love life to have created in each living being such a strong drive to continue to live. Death may be natural, but life still vies against it; and that is as God intended.

Houston 3

During supper today, Houston died. Andrew said, "I'll get the shovels, and you wrap her up." In a few minutes we met out at the hole by the compost pile that Rob had already dug. Andrew took Houston, wrapped in a baby blanket, and placed her in the hole; and we began to put dirt on the body. But something just didn't seem right. Andrew said, "Mom, what if she's not really dead yet, but just unconscious? She'll suffocate." I said, "Do you want to take her back in and check?" He nodded, so I lifted the body out of the hole, and we headed back to the house.

We examined the body carefully. Then Andrew said, "I think we need a box." So we went down to the basement to find the perfect box. "Mom, let's put some things in the box, something valuable, like money." "But money wasn't valuable to Houston." We settled for some dry cat food, sprinkles of water, and a turkey wishbone. "How about putting in a picture of the kittens?" We spent a long time looking for a picture of the kittens and at all the other pictures.

In a much calmer, satisfied mood, we returned to the gravesite. Placing the box in the hole, we filled in the dirt. It was a moonless, starry night, and Andrew and I shoveled the dirt more by feel than sight. It was quiet and majestic, and God seemed close. Andrew summed it all up when he said, "It's really nice out here tonight." And it was. Houston made me think about my memorial service someday. I want it to be personal, thoughtful, unhurried, and filled with divine wonder, so that people there may leave feeling, "It is really nice to be here today."

Tomatoes 1

In August and September tomatoes are plentiful. We have sliced tomatoes with almost every lunch and dinner. They are red, ripe, and luscious. I send Andrew out to the garden to pick one right before dinner is ready. I slice it, still warm from the sunshine, and we eat it when it's at its peak of flavor. I remember mother scraping any leftover tomato slices into the bucket of vegetable leavings headed back to the garden to enrich the soil. It was the only table leftovers my mother ever "threw away." Wasting food was not in her nature. She explained that once a tomato is sliced, the air and the refrigerator change its flavor so quickly it's not worth saving when tomatoes are plentiful.

At the food pantry today I was carefully laying out our tomatoes. A little boy came trotting over and picked up a beautiful red, ripe tomato. His mother quickly said, "Oh, not that one, it's much too soft. We must squeeze the tomatoes and find one that's nice and firm. A firm one will keep while that one you picked will spoil right away." With that she searched around until she found a greener tomato and happily added it to her food order.

It made me sad. Although the ripe tomato won't keep as long as the greener one, the greener tomato doesn't have that wonderful garden-ripe flavor. It also saddened me to think that firm, green, grocery-store tomatoes have become the standard of excellence. Have we really come so far away from our lives as farmers and gatherers? Is garden-ripened produce to be less prized than packaged foods? As I slice my sun-warmed, ripe tomato for lunch, I sincerely hope not.

Thanks

Yesterday we returned from a wonderful camping trip on the beach of Lake Michigan. We hiked and biked, swam and built fires, and picked up lots of rocks. Last night I knew I should go out to the garden to pick the vegetables. Jerie had picked while we were gone, but it was time again. Certainly the squash needed picking if we wished to avoid squash three feet long. Unfortunately, after a week of no such responsibilities, I didn't want to go. Finally, with a very grudging attitude, grumbling all the while about the foolishness of doing such a big garden anyway, I went out and picked the harvest.

Today Andrew and I headed out to deliver our produce. First stop was Kumler United Methodist Church, our neighborhood pantry. They welcomed us, asked about our vacation, and thanked us for arranging for them to get harvest while we were gone. At Christ Episcopal's pantry, Jackie greeted us, "I missed you last week. I have something for you. Rob wouldn't let me send you a thank-you note, but he can't keep me from giving you one." She handed me a thank-you poster along with a big smile.

Andrew and I came home smiling, renewed, and feeling the garden was important and worth the effort. Although Jesus said to do your charity in secret, I admit to having the need for simple thanks. Often the appreciation of others helps to fill my heart up again. We do not live in secret; we live in community, and when the community supports our efforts, it is far easier to carry on. So I have hung my thank-you poster on the refrigerator, where I can see it whenever I pass.

First of the Month

I wish we could train our garden to produce with the calendar in mind. Last week at the pantry Kathy said to us, "We can use everything you have to bring, as it will go quickly." This week I took tomatoes in on Wednesday and was surprised to see that the produce table still held some of the vegetables we had brought in Monday. The difference between last week and this week is that the calendar has changed. Last week was the end of the month when many families run out of money and food. Last week the food pantry was filled with people in need.

This week is the first of the month. Disability, welfare, and Social Security checks have come. A new supply of food stamps has been issued. The local discount grocery is filled. Carts are piled high with food—food people hope will last to the end of the month. Everybody eats the first of the month. So our garden produce is not in such great demand. I wish I were able to speak to my plants and ask them to hold off their harvest for a week. Next week, food orders will again be needed. As the month passes, the stream will steadily grow. By the end of the month a flood of need will again pass through the food pantry.

At times I get overwhelmed by the amount of poverty and problems right here in our community. I get discouraged that there is little I can do to make a difference. And at times the efforts of government and social services don't seem to be sufficient. In such times I have to remember that at least in this community, in this country, everybody eats at the first of the month.

Watermelons 1

This year we planted watermelons in the space just vacated by the spinach and lettuce. We don't weed our watermelons because they need to hide—first from the hot sun and second from the neighborhood kids. Raiding a neighbor's watermelons is an American tradition and seems an irresistible part of childhood. So we allow the crabgrass to grow up and hide the growing melons. Sometimes thievery is a strange help! The broken remains of a watermelon help solve the garden's main mystery: "Are the watermelons ripe?!?" It is hard to choose a ripe watermelon in the grocery. It is even harder to decide when to pick a watermelon in the garden. They show no telltale turning of color or any other exterior sign. The only true test is to cut it open. Unfortunately, once it is cut, it cannot be made to ripen further.

Two weeks ago, Rob chose a small watermelon. It was still mostly white inside, but was faintly sweet and surprisingly refreshing. Today, Rob cut another one. It should have been riper, having had two more weeks in the sun, but it was still green. Unfortunately, we have only one *big* melon in the patch. We would like to pick it at just the right time. The mystery remains: Is it ripe yet? The only way to know is to cut it.

How like some of life's biggest decisions our watermelons are! No distinct sign reveals the perfect time to marry, to have a child, to retire, to move, or to change jobs. One must make the best judgment and then move ahead in faith. If later the decision proves to have been premature, not quite ripe, we hope we can still find it surprisingly sweet.

Watermelons 2

Yesterday, we picked all the rest of the melons, and I cut one open for supper. It split at the touch of the knife, was bright pink, and smelled delicious. In short, it seemed perfect. I piled the pieces on a platter. Strangely enough, when Andrew cleared the table, we had almost a full platter of watermelon left. Why? They looked wonderful but tasted rather flat. How strange! When they looked green and flavorless, we were surprised to find them sweet. Now, they look ripe and sweet, but lack flavor.

Often our expectations have more to do with our satisfaction than does the actual experience. Today Andrew and I walked to raise money for the food relief branch of Church World Service. Each year Andrew has proved me wrong in my prediction. The first year, at age five, I expected Andrew to walk one mile—he went three miles. Last year, I predicted five kilometers—he walked the entire ten. This year he and I both thought ten would be no problem. Again we were wrong. His legs started to hurt, and a blister on his heel appeared, so at seven kilometers we headed for the finish. We were both disappointed. How ridiculous not to feel happy and proud! Seven kilometers is still a long way for a seven–year-old to walk. We still raised a large sum for the world's hungry. The only reason for our disappointment was our expectation!

It is the same with our watermelons. The only reason they don't taste sweet is because we expect them to taste sweeter.

Endings

This first Saturday of autumn, Jerie beat me out to the garden. Seeing her, I slipped into my garden shoes and quickly followed. Jerie was sort of wandering around the edge of the garden. When I joined her, we stood there with hands on hips. Finally, I said, "Well, I guess we'd better do this." She answered, "I guess we had." We both took a bag and waded in to pick tomatoes. A few minutes later, Andrew burst out of the house and ran up saying, "Anything I can do?"

"You can pick the green peppers."

Looking at the garden, now overgrown with crabgrass, he said, "No, I don't think so," turned, and ran back to the house. Jerie and I laughed. We knew exactly how he felt. Without a sense of obligation and a wish not to waste food, we, too, would have turned heel and left. Soon we will close the garden, and frankly we are looking forward to the end.

Each year I am reminded that endings are just as important as beginnings. We've had our best garden this year, but now it is finishing. The plants are dead or dying, the harvest is gone or dwindling, and our interest and energy is waning. The ground and I both need a change. However, I celebrate this ending rather than grieve for it. This ending and the following winter break will allow me to plant again next spring. If gardens did not end, I doubt that I would plant at all. I need the ending to relish the beginning again.

God was very wise to have filled our world with endings. God was very wise to have created the night, the seasons, the Sabbath, and the stages of our lives.

Tomatoes 2

This afternoon, out of curiosity, I took the bathroom scales out to the garage and weighed the tomatoes we had picked this morning. I calculated the weight of each bag and the crop totaled seventy-five pounds! Not a bad haul, considering it is the second week in October.

One tomato plant of our forty has been particularly amazing. For the last three Saturdays, I have picked one whole bag, about ten pounds of tomatoes, off this one plant. Curious as to today's yield, I started with that plant and was amazed to find another half bag of harvest. The plant now looks brown and dried and thoroughly spent, but has yielded at least thirty-five pounds of food in four pickings.

I've also been watching the plant next to my high-producer. It looks so healthy, green and bushy; but each week we have found only three or four ripe tomatoes on it. Today again, the plant yielded only a few to pick, but I noticed that it is now loaded with green tomatoes. Unfortunately, frost may come this week, and we plan to pull up all the tomato plants this coming Sunday. My green, healthy bush spent too much time getting ready, and now it is just too late.

I wonder in what ways I am like my second tomato plant?

What dreams am I putting off?

What calls to faithfulness am I postponing?

What challenges or ministries are ones that I am not yet ready for?

I must be alert, for the frost is coming, and then it will be too late.

Twenty-six Weeks

Twenty-six weeks ago we took our first offering, our thank offering, of radishes and lettuce to the food pantry. For twenty-six weeks the garden has produced a bounty of food as the vegetables rapidly succeeded each other. For twenty-six weeks we have also reaped the harvest of friendship from the garden. Friends came to plant. Jerie has come to help every Saturday morning, and each Monday we've been greeted with smiles when we brought in our food. Today we asked a few friends to help us close the garden. Seventy tomato cages are now stacked in the shed. Five boxes of green tomatoes are carefully packed to ripen in the darkness. Only the stalks and stubble are left waiting to freeze and return to the soil. Over the coming months the quiet magic of decay will occur, and the ground will again be tilled to a smooth bed of fresh, crumbly, brown dirt ready to receive the seeds. In twenty-six weeks we will again have a thank offering.

> For everything there is a season, and a time for every
>   matter under heaven:
> a time to be born, and a time to die;
> a time to plant, and a time to pluck up what is planted;
> a time to kill, and a time to heal;
> a time to break down, and a time to build up;…
> a time to seek, and a time to lose;
> a time to keep, and a time to throw away;…
> a time to love, and a time to hate;
> a time for war, and a time for peace.
>   ECCLESIASTES 3:1–3, 6, 8

God has made everything beautiful in its time.

third season

Thought Time

I haven't written anything all winter. The tasks of the day filled my time, and I gave any leisure time over to reading or resting or being with Rob and Andrew. But now that the days are longer and the garden is again lush, I find my mind brimming and my pen speeding. My mind is full of new musings because my gardening time is when my thoughts are most free. My hands are busy, but my brain can wander lazily, or dance joyfully, or seek prayerfully.

I wonder if old-time hobbies like embroidery, knitting, or whittling were really all about freedom of thought—a chance to free the mind while the hands are kept occupied. How else can you explain embroidery on the underwear of women who had to grow, spin, and weave their own cloth? Or why else did men who cleared their land with an ax elaborately carve simple tools such as pie crimpers?

Maybe the loss of such "thought time" contributes to why so many modern people suffer from stress. Modern relaxations, like movies, computers, video games, TV, and radio rest the body but keep the mind occupied. We have little or no time to busy our hands or body and thereby free our minds to rest or frolic, and free our spirits to dream and be renewed. This time of garden meditation goes even deeper for me. As I touch the ground, I touch again that which grounds me: my convictions and beliefs, my memories and dreams, and my thoughts of people in my life. In short, I rediscover in the garden the reasons why I get up every day. Recognizing my need for thought time, I offer these simple movements of my mind for a third season.

Power Gardens

This week's news magazine has an article on "power gardening." It claims that gardens are the latest status rage. Frankly, I grew incensed just glancing through the pictures.

- Gardening is not about designer outfits, high-tech knee pads, and $2,000 trowels. It is about old clothes, rusty tools, and muddy knees.
- Gardening is not about fashion and appearances. It is about quiet mornings alone when no one sees you.
- Gardening is not about control and order. It is about experiencing the natural processes beyond our making, seeing the interplay of plants with weather, insects, water, and soil.
- Gardening is not about transplanting full-sized trees or already blooming roses. It is about planting something that looks dead and hoping for its transformation.
- Gardening is not about competition. It is about participating in creation.
- Gardening is not about exotic fads. It is about roots, both literally and figuratively.

After my ire waned, I decided to read the article. It concludes with the belief that in the end, gardens captivate their gardeners and exert their virtues on their "owners," for we never really own a garden. My response was "Amen!" When human beings believe we "own" the land and control nature, God's creation, we put the survival of all life at risk.

Garden Party

For the past three years we have sent invitations to a garden party (translation: garden*ing* party) in celebration of May Day, my birthday. The first year it sprinkled, the second year it was rained out...twice. This year the day was bright and sunny, perfect for planting. Fourteen friends came to plant: friends from church, friends from the neighborhood, friends from Rob's work, and friends from Andrew's school. Rob and I were kept hopping just directing it all. In two hours, everything was planted and all the black plastic was laid. We were thrilled to have it completed!

These last few weeks have confirmed what a special gift our friends have given us. For three solid weeks, work schedules and heavy thunderstorms have kept us from doing any more work in the garden. Had our friends not come and given of themselves, of their time, and of their muscles, we might not have a garden at all this spring.

A dozen years ago, Rob and I lost a baby through miscarriage. Unfortunately, we had kept my pregnancy secret and thus kept the loss a secret, too. We shut out the support we badly needed, and the experience became like a festering wound in our lives. Had we opened ourselves to our friends, healing would have come much more quickly. How much better are our lives when we live in community. How much better are our lives when we make friendship a priority. That is the support we all need. Unfortunately, that support can only come when we open ourselves to seek and accept it.

Our friends gave me a wonderful birthday present, but I had to offer the invitation and ask them to come.

Leaf Tatter

For several weeks this May we've had wild thunderstorms, so we could do little more than wander out to the garden between storms to see how the plants were faring. The answer was, "Not too well!" Many of the plants were full of tiny holes. We couldn't see any apparent insects, but I dusted the plants with insecticide anyway, only to have the next rain wash away my efforts.

Unable to cure the problem, I simply resorted to worry. Being anxious is something I practice often. Rob reminds me that worry is not in keeping with being a "mediocre gardener." A mediocre gardener rejoices at whatever grows and bears fruit, and shrugs off whatever dies, rots, or is eaten by insects. I know he is right, but my fretting continues.

This morning, Jerie told me she had read in the paper about "leaf tatter." Although I had never heard of it, apparently many gardens have suffered from it this year. Leaf tatter looks like insect damage, but it is really damage caused by high winds pulverizing the plants with tiny dirt particles. My insecticide was useless against leaf tatter…as useless as my fretting.

Some of the plants have died and will need to be replaced. Some appear to be stunted. But some are thriving. In each case, my worry had no effect on their survival. To paraphrase Matthew 6:27, my anxiety added not one hour to the lifespan of anything in my garden.

Saturday

This morning I got up and, like a robot, pulled on my garden clothes. I drank my coffee and wandered out to our plot. Though still in a sleepy trance, I set to work pulling weeds.

Slowly I awakened to the peace and beauty around me. The birds were singing, the air was fresh and cool, and the sunlight was filtered and kind. With gladness I rejoiced at being present there.

I could be out in the garden any morning—nothing prevents me—but somehow, other tasks, preoccupations, or simple laziness crowd in, and I stay in the house or race away in the car.

But today is different. Today is Saturday: the day Jerie comes over, the morning we garden, the morning when gardening is a habit. Had I not predetermined that this time would be set aside for this task, most likely I would have missed this morning and its beauty.

I feel the same way about attending church. Many people who do not align themselves with a congregation say that they can worship God in their own way and experience God in God's creation. I suppose that may be possible. Unfortunately, I need the weekly habit to make God's presence real in my life, not just a possibility.

Were I not in the Saturday habit, I would surely miss some beautiful mornings...and the weeds would undoubtedly flourish.

Were I not in the Sunday habit, I would surely miss some of God's leading...and spiritual weeds would also flourish.

Lettuce

This morning, Andrew came into our bedroom and jumped on us at 5:45 a.m. "Come on! Get up! You said we wanted to get out to the garden early." (Well, not that early!) In response we struggled out of bed, grabbed our coffee, and stumbled around. Despite our efforts with breakfast and entreaty, we couldn't keep Andrew from dancing around eagerly. Soon we gave him a knife, the key to the tool shed, and permission to start out ahead of us. Why all the excitement about going out to the garden? Well, today Andrew gets to "lumberman" the lettuce. We have been taking lettuce to the food pantries for several weeks, but very soon it will all be bitter from the hot sun. It is time to harvest it or see it wasted. So today, Andrew can cut, cut, cut! We will have a big load of lettuce to take to The Breadline, where free meals are served twice a day.

By the time Rob and I had followed Andrew to the garden this morning, he had already filled several big buckets and was happily chopping away. By the time he quit and ran inside for his allotted TV, Andrew had filled five big garbage bags and left the lettuce patch looking bare and plundered. For energetic kids like Andrew, lettuce is a most satisfying crop. The planting is fun since you can fling and scatter the seeds broadly. Then the seeds sprout into little green dots and are fun to watch as school winds down. When first harvested, you can pick it like a bouquet, some of every kind, and even taste it a little. Then, finally, one summer day you can just ravage it with abandon and have your parents' approval! Indeed, lettuce must be the perfect children's crop.

Sheep Sorrel

When I was a little girl, I used to delight in finding sheep sorrel in the yard. I loved to pluck and eat it. It has a sweet flavor with just a touch of sour. In fact, I remember I used to call it "sweet and sour," although my mom called it "sheep sorrel" (or was it "sheep's sorrow"?).

Whatever its name, when we returned to Illinois, I showed the plant to Andrew. It is easy to recognize: it has three small heart-shaped leaves, tiny yellow flowers like forget-me-nots, and a bright spring-green color. Andrew, who will eat very few vegetables, was intrigued by the idea of eating a weed. He was even more surprised to find he liked the taste. I mean, really liked it! Now, whenever he spots sheep sorrel, I find him munching away.

He has introduced it to April and other kids in the neighborhood. Indeed, sheep sorrel has become the official food of their "Multi Club." The Multi Club has its own garden right next to their clubhouse, and into it Andrew and April have lovingly planted the seed pods of sheep sorrel.

I wonder what the vitamin and mineral content of sheep sorrel is. I assume being green and growing, it must have some. I am just glad Andrew has finally found some vegetable he really likes, even if I can't buy it in the grocery. It makes me laugh to think about all our efforts to get him to try "regular" food.

Hmmm…Do you suppose I can freeze some for the winter?

Cherries

A bowl of cherries sits on a shelf in my refrigerator waiting for me to cook them into something sweet and delicious. Every time I open the refrigerator, the cherries seem to look up at me expectantly. But each day, they look a little less rosy, as their freshness seeps away. I muse that it would take only a little time and effort to turn them into something good to eat; but deep down, I admit they are probably headed for the compost pile.

Why have I left them to spoil, making me feel guilty and wasteful? First, the temperature is very hot, and I am reluctant to turn on the stove or oven for any reason. Meals are made straight from the refrigerator or using only the toaster, grill, or microwave. Second and more important, I have chosen to spend my summer time playing with Andrew—reading aloud, swimming, pitching, talking, or just being together.

A long list of house projects is posted in the kitchen. Only a few things have been crossed off, and this summer will result in only a couple more deletions. The fact is: every summer will have its own house mending projects. I can cook cherries anytime, but only *this* summer will our son be eight years old.

Consequently, the cherries in the refrigerator will go to feed the birds or enrich the earth. However, they have already served my purpose because Andrew and I had fun picking them from the tree, and we will remember that time together.

third season

Radish-in-a-Rock 1

This morning while I was pulling radishes, one came out surrounded by a stone. The many good-sized rocks in our garden are full of holes. My radish had found its way through one of those holes. I'm sure it wiggled through as a slender root, and then grew and expanded, and bulged out on both sides of the hole. The rock once had trapped the radish, but now the radish has trapped the rock.

We all looked at the radish in wonder and delight. When we came in, Rob plopped it in a jar of water, hoping to revive it. Unfortunately, having been pulled from the ground, its ability to draw water was damaged, so it remained limp.

But Rob's instinct to preserve it was the right one. Surely such perseverance is to be honored. For me, the radish-in-a-rock perfectly illustrates the meaning of the saying: "Flourish where you are planted."

Many of us find things in our lives that seem like boulders blocking our way. Those blocks may be childhood experiences, grief, physical disabilities, or poor choices in the past. Somehow, with God's leading, we must find our way through that blockage so we can continue to grow and produce.

Radish-in-a-Rock 2

For a few days, the radish-in-a-rock sat in its glass of water, half-forgotten on the kitchen table. It was waiting to be thrown onto the compost pile. Then, slowly, as it waited, a strange thing happened: the droopy stem began to straighten, and the leaves began to perk up. The plant had begun to take in water.

I was amazed when I rediscovered the renewed radish-in-a-rock…amazed at the will of life to sustain itself.

When I weed, I always just let the weeds lie where they are pulled, thus adding to the mulch. Rob, on the other hand, carefully takes the weeds to the compost pile, claiming, "They can reroot themselves." I have always laughed at that notion and said, "They cannot!" "Sure they can, just look at the weeds growing out of the compost pile." I just shake my head and laugh again. Now looking at my radish-in-a-rock, I'm not so certain.

Can weeds really replant themselves?

Is it possible that weeds in my life can also replant themselves? Are the anxieties, temptations, and habits that I think I have disposed of not really dead? If given the right conditions, will they take hold again? On the other hand, is it possible that opportunities that I think are gone forever can come again, if I keep aware?

I still believe that weeds, once pulled up and cast aside, are dead; but I will be more vigilant. In the meantime, I plan to hunt up a pot for the radish-in-a-rock and see if it really is going to make it. I hope so.

Radishes

The radishes have been a mysterious disappointment this year. We first planted radishes in April. Our spring was cool and wet—seemingly, the perfect weather for radishes. But the radishes turned woody, bitter, and hot as jalapeño peppers. Why, with perfect conditions for growing, were they bad? The second batch planted in mid-May promised to be much better. At the first picking, the radishes were crisp and sweet—perfect for eating. But…then the dry heat of June descended, and the radish plants sprouted tall tops and woody roots. The few radishes found were split and dry and again fiery hot.

Today, I pulled up all the remaining radish plants, finding only a small handful of good radishes. I wondered why they failed. Did we plant them too thickly? Possibly. However, in a few places the radishes were equally crowded, and each plant grew a fat radish, almost as if they had encouraged each other to produce. I thought about our life in New York City some years ago. People are crowded together and stacked on top of one another. The worst conditions of human life are magnified: poverty, crime, racism, fear, and hatred. But you also find the opportunity for people from many cultures and lands to live together as neighbors and friends, to appreciate each other and the richness of our world. The gathering of artists, musicians, scientists, and scholars trading ideas results in an unrivaled bubbling of creativity. Few things in this world are straightforward and simple. Most things in life are like my radishes: complicated, confusing, and tinged with mystery.

Broccoli

We have an anomaly in the garden this year: a volunteer broccoli. It appeared on its own and is now about to produce a head.

Today looking at it I realize that, although I have been around gardens for most of my life, I have never seen a volunteer broccoli. In fact, I don't know what a broccoli seed looks like or how it comes up as a sprout. I buy broccoli plants as young seedlings after someone else has planted and nurtured the seeds.

It started me thinking about all the ways I am dependent on other people's knowledge and effort. Someone else has made virtually everything in my house somewhere else, through processes that I little understand.

Perhaps that is why gardening holds such value for me. I can be part of the entire process of growth, from the sprouting of the seed to the withering of the plant. That puts me closer to an understanding of God's creation than anything else I touch. Each year I am in awe at the growth process: it is intricate yet flexible, specific yet interconnected, fragile yet tenacious. Such complexity could not be by accident. Instead it reveals to me a Creator who is caring and wise beyond my capacity to understand.

Salty 1

A white cat is meowing in my garage tonight, and I am in a dilemma as to what to do. This is a young cat, partly grown, partly kitten. It appeared in our garage two days ago and has not ventured more than a few feet since. It seems frightened—not of people, but rather of its situation. It's hungry and lost, and, I suspect, out-of-doors for the first time. I am angry at the unknown person who dropped this cat at my doorstep. Yet I can understand why they might. With an average of 70,000 puppies and kittens born each day, it is difficult to find homes for them.

What are the alternatives if you can't find a home? The animal shelter stays full; setting kittens free in the woods is death either for the kittens or for the songbirds; and taking them to the pound often means death by injection. So, someone has dropped this kitty here, hoping a family will take it in.

I know if I feed it, it will stay, and I don't wish for another cat, but its cries as a hurting creature of God cut into me.

I am reminded of similar feelings of conflict and discomfort when I meet a person of need on the street. My desire to help conflicts with my fear for my safety. My distress that I might slight someone who sincerely needs aid conflicts with my distrust that I am being conned. I fear involvement, but I cannot simply pass by.

The cat continues to meow in the garage, and I am left with a dilemma that makes any decision uncomfortable.

Salty 2

The white cat stayed. At the request of the Humane Society we started feeding her until they could find a new home for her. Little did I realize that the new home would be ours! She has slowly become our cat.

She has a name, Salty, a natural choice since we already have a cat named Pepper. Unfortunately, Pepper does not want a soul mate. Pepper now asks to be let in and out of the front door, thus avoiding Salty. Likewise, Salty will not come into the house, Pepper's house. She will venture out to the garden or join our neighbors on their porch, but mostly she stays in the garage. A sweet and playful cat, she looks very refined with pure white fur and golden eyes. When I stoop to pick her up, I sense her untamed nature. Her beautiful white hair feels coarse like a wild animal's pelt.

When we returned from our vacation, her side bulges showed that Salty is pregnant. I had worried about having one outdoor cat. Now I worry we will have a whole litter of outdoor kittens. They will be wild, and thus impossible to find homes for. We seem to be faced with the same decision that Salty's previous owner faced. Should we take the kittens to the woods, to the pound...or...should we drop them off in a family neighborhood and hope that they will be adopted? How often I wish I could take back words and thoughts of criticism, criticism that I made because I had never faced the same situation. Before I was a parent, I said many times, "If I were that child's mother, I wouldn't allow him to act that way." Now I am a parent, and I understand the difficult tasks and choices facing mothers. Now I repent of my criticism.

Salty 3

The questions about Salty and her kittens will never be answered, for she has disappeared as suddenly as she appeared. Part of me is relieved, but that doesn't keep me from walking the neighborhood, calling her name. So far she has not been found. Although her presence was unsought and brought problems and worry, I now grieve at her absence.

I suspect she may have gotten into a car, perhaps our car, and accidentally been driven to another place. Several times, I discovered her lounging in the car. Instead of meowing when the motor started, she hid. Possibly this last time, I didn't see her scurry under the seat. Maybe unwittingly, I dropped her off in another neighborhood. If so, I hope it was a family neighborhood, and I hope she finds a new home.

This week two of the people I had grown to know and appreciate disappeared from the homeless shelter where Rob and I work. Nora had been so excited to get an Illinois ID and to start class at the Adult Education Center. She and Curt seemed to have a good chance of finding a more stable life here in Springfield.

Then, as suddenly and as inexplicably as Salty, they disappeared and moved on to places unknown. I understand we will not be able to positively affect everyone's life, but that does not keep me from grieving the loss of these two people. I hope somewhere, sometime, they may catch hold of a place and decide to stay and make it their home.

Chickweed

This morning, Karen and April came to the door all excited. "The eggs have hatched!" I immediately went with them back to their house. Their canary birds had a nest of eggs and now two tiny chicks, no bigger than my thumbnail. Karen and I started talking about food for the babies. I suggested they put some chickweed in the cage for the parents. "What's chickweed?" asked April. She and I went looking for some in the yard to bring back for the birds. I haven't picked chickweed in probably twenty-five years. It set me to remembering the various parakeets I have known. Blue Boy of my childhood used to chatter up a storm from his cage, and peck any finger that ventured near. My family gave my grandmother Pretty Bird to keep her company. Grandma talked a lot to it, and it learned to mimic her.

Critter came into our life our first year of marriage. An unusually smart parakeet, he quickly learned how to open his cage door. Despite our efforts, he continually escaped the cage. Finally, we left the door open and gave him the freedom of the house. He loved to push things off of tables, peck the water from atop the shower head, roll around on the floor with a rubber band, and talk to the birds outside the window. He showed annoyance by making great, zooming circles of flight—upstairs, downstairs, and back upstairs. Critter added much merriment to our lives.

My thoughts about the birds in my past made me realize again how much my life and memories are filled with relationships. Whom I have known and what we've experienced together form the greatest importance and value to me.

Treasures

Often after a thunderstorm, we find interesting things popping up from the soil in the garden.

Today was extraordinarily rewarding. Rob found a plastic man dated 1983. Jerie found three pieces of pottery together in a clod of dirt. They were blue and white porcelain and almost paper thin...remarkably delicate. I found a chunk of deep purple glass, the bottom of a bottle, with a mysterious imprint of letters. I also found a pure white pebble, smooth and rounded as from a rock tumbler. Surely at some point it lay for a long time in a riverbed, rolling over and over.

But the most intriguing find was a small sphere. It's too round to seem natural, but what is it? It has some rough spots like a clinker, but also some smooth spots like glazing. Andrew suggested it was a steel ball bearing that had corroded. "Or," he said, "maybe it is a marble that got burned in a fire." We have tried scrubbing it, scratching it, and soaking it in vinegar; but there has been no change. I think it looks like a glob of lava that exploded out of a volcano and solidified in the air. But how did a piece of lava come to be buried in Illinois?

How did any of these treasures come to our garden? Who was the child who lost the plastic man? Who drank from the fine china teacup? What was held in the purple bottle? Where was the river of the tumbled rock? Our garden holds mysteries of history and geology and brings a sense of connection with times past.

Peonies

When we lived in Kentucky, I read about a bequest of peonies to Henry Clay's home. The gift was applauded because the peonies were many decades old. We had peonies in the yard when I was growing up—big, beautiful flowers in the middle of the lawn, teeming with ants. Across the street in a vacant lot three large stands of peonies—red, white, and pink—have bloomed proudly for untold decades. Last fall, someone bought the lot to build a new house. The owner said I could have the peonies if I was willing to transplant them. I planned to do so in the spring. In January renters moved into the house adjacent to the lot—renters with loud music, foul language, and a yard strewn with liquor bottles. I and my neighbors felt invaded and disgusted. Our anger turned to fear as it became more and more obvious they were selling drugs. Gunfire was heard, and a rottweiler took up residence to ward off unwanted visitors.

With the spring, the neighborhood petitioned to rid itself of these persons. Simultaneously, the peonies came up. The renters stayed. It was time to transplant, but my sense of vulnerability kept me on my side of the street. The peonies bloomed. Now the renters have finally moved, but it is too late to transplant the peonies. Today the dark red blossoms were buried under the foundation of the new house, and the white ones will soon disappear beneath the driveway. I am saddened to see this heritage of perhaps half a century destroyed. A spot of beauty for the whole neighborhood is gone—destroyed by the ugliness of a few persons.

third season

Catalogs

My father used to say, "You are fully adult when you can't find anything in the Sears™ catalog that you want." As a child, I used to wonder at that statement. I could pore over the thick book and long for dozens of things! Could one ever get to the point of not wanting something from the Sears™ catalog?

We no longer get the Sears™ catalog, and the few catalogs that arrive in the mail hold little magic for me. I guess I am fully grown up, as now I can quickly flip through a catalog without even a fleeting interest in anything.

However…last year when Rob began to care for his mother's finances, all her mail was diverted to our house. Along came various flower catalogs, catalogs filled with beautiful pictures of poppies, irises, roses, and peonies. The catalogs proclaim: "Save 37% if you order by June 1st." "Get 6 bleeding hearts, *free*." "Everything is fully guaranteed to grow to your satisfaction!"

Ah! The wonder of catalogs has returned for me. I now have a special file among my "important" papers for flower catalogs. I pore over them on pretense of finding the best buy, but really I am setting my imagination churning. I can just see various beauties in my yard, and I am ready to replace all the weed spots.

Give me a cup of coffee, a piece of quiet to myself, and a flower catalog. Then I will wander through the beautiful pictures, gaze at the exotic blooms from around the world, and dream longingly, desiring them all. I guess I'm still a kid after all!

Tulips and Daffodils

Yesterday while swimming at the beach, I felt something on my foot. Lifting it out of the water, I discovered a ten-dollar bill. After much family discussion about its possible uses, I ordered tulip bulbs, the expensive collection with the black tulips.

I think there is something faithful about buying and planting perennials like tulips. It is a statement of belief in the future and hope for good things to come. Many perennials grace our yard. Each spring we enjoy anew the daffodils, tulips, bluebells, and trilliums. Each summer we greet irises, daylilies, spiderwort, and roses. Mrs. Webb probably planted most of them. She lived here for four decades. Here her children grew, and here her life unfolded as year after year the perennials appeared and bloomed. But it might be that some of the flowers go all the way back to the woman who built this house nearly a century ago.

We have a friend who built a new home in the woods of Kentucky. In the fall she planted a dozen daffodil bulbs down in the woods. When spring came, she was amazed to see hundreds of daffodils. At first she thought her few bulbs had magically multiplied. But then she realized a cabin must have stood down in the woods. The woman who lived there planted the daffodils, perhaps just a dozen at first. In planting them, she made a statement about home, about permanence, and about dreams. The cabin is long gone, but the daffodils remain, each spring spreading their message of hope.

Shade Garden

For the first couple of years in this house, we planted grass seed in our front yard, only to see it wash away, or wither away, or simply never sprout. By midsummer we would resign ourselves to a lawn of mud and chickweed. An arborist friend pointed to our big maple tree that shades the entire front yard as the problem: "You will never have grass, not just because of the shade, but also because of the essential natures of maples and grass. Grass likes alkaline soil; maples like it acid. In such a mineral battle both can't win. Over the years the maple has probably drained the soil of its other nutrients, using them to produce its great canopy of leaves."

Last fall Andrew bought a soil testing kit at a garage sale, and we proceeded to test the front dirt. Sure enough, the soil registered the worst possible for every mineral tested—no nitrogen, no potash, no phosphorous, but great quantities of acid. Convinced that grass was futile, I ordered a "shade garden" of acid-loving plants. Andrew and I lovingly unpacked the hostas, ferns, lilies, and forget-me-nots. I spaded, fertilized, planted, and mulched. Everyday I pause to check the progress. This morning, five lily blossoms: two pink, two white, and one orange greeted me—like five stars shining just for me.

Flowers grace my yard because I sought my friend's counsel and trusted his advice. Likewise, faith in God includes seeking God's truth, asking the questions that lead to God's will, and trusting that God is with us. Only then can we perceive the grace of God in our lives and the stars of blessing that God has planted there.

Gardenias

Today I threw away my potted gardenia. It was mostly dead with just a few green leaves. I bought it last Valentine's Day, seeking the joy of blooming flowers in the midst of winter. I considered the iris and the hyacinths, but kept returning to a gardenia plant covered with buds. The florist said it would bloom in a few days. I went home feeling very springy and romantic. I could almost smell the sweet perfume of the delicate white flowers. I thought of the time Rob surprised me with a gardenia corsage. I remembered a friend's yard with a gardenia bush as big as a tree; its smell was like a magic spell cast over the entire house. I hoped my gardenia would send its sweetness to each and every corner of our home.

But soon the buds turned brown and dropped off. I thought maybe the cold car ride had affected them. Undaunted, I carefully watered and fertilized the plant. Soon I was rewarded with a new crop of buds. Again I waited for the flowers and the smell; again the buds died unopened. I decided the house might be too cold at night. Not despairing, I tended the plant and waited for summer. Summer brought a new crop of buds, but no flowers. Discouraged, today I discarded my gardenia hopes.

Not everything we attempt will turn out as we dream. Despite our best efforts, businesses fail, children make bad choices, friends fall away, and our bodies become frail. We cannot control the outcome; we can only control our input and our attitudes. My gardenia never bloomed, but it will be sad if my experience with it keeps me from buying February flowers again.

Bleeding Hearts

This afternoon, Andrew and Rob took off on an adventure, giving me a piece of time to myself. I decided to plant some perennials that arrived this week: daylilies, lilies of the valley, and pink bleeding hearts. As I planted, I observed the people passing by.

First, our neighbor Eric came strolling out of his house. I asked about his mother, who has been in the hospital for two months. "She's trying another new medicine, and we hope it will help." Second, a slow-moving old car stopped, and a woman with tears rolling down her face asked, "Have you seen a three-year-old boy come this way? I only left him outside for a minute while I went to check on the other children. Now I can't find him." Third, two teenagers strolled by, and a snippet of their conversation came to my ears. "I'd never let any bitch treat me that way; I'd beat her ass to a pulp." Fourth, an old man came walking slowly down the street with a tiny girl, maybe three years old. They were carrying grocery bags. They passed me and continued on down the next block.

Am I really grateful enough for all the simple blessings in my life, things I so often take for granted: my health, my relationships, and my possessions? I can't truly imagine life as a mentally ill or physically handicapped person, or life as a single parent, or life with an abusive partner, or even life without my trusty transportation. Surely goodness and mercy are following me all the days of my life (Ps. 23).

While planting (and observing) bleeding hearts today, I was overwhelmed with gratitude and compassion.

Grocery Thoughts 1

Yesterday a young mother's cart caught my attention and admiration. It contained only basic food—flour, sugar, shortening, fresh fruits and vegetables, macaroni, cottage cheese, and some canned goods—no sweets or prepared foods. Whatever cookies or cakes her family ate, she must have made herself from scratch. I noticed food stamps in her hand, as did another woman in line. This other woman began to examine critically the basket I had just admired and immediately switched her conversation to those "awful people" who abuse food stamps. In a loud voice, she asked, "Why is she buying canned beans? Why doesn't she buy dried beans and cook them herself?"

I had to intervene. "Excuse me; have you ever cooked beans in the summer with no air conditioning? I cook beans in the winter to heat up my whole house." That quieted the woman long enough for all of us to check out. The young mother was buying plain, nutritious food and doing it at the cheapest grocery in town. She was using her food stamps in the way I wish all recipients would use them. But simply because she had food stamps, the other woman was going to find something to criticize.

Often we fall into the mindset of the "other woman," afraid someone might get something for nothing. If they haven't earned it with their labor, they must "earn" it by suffering our scorn and our accusations. In the process we strip people of whatever pride they have left. We strip ourselves of the joy of helping. If we think only of their taking, then we have lost the spirit of gratitude in our giving.

Grocery Thoughts 2

In Kentucky, we lived across the street from an active African American church. The people dressed "to the nines." On certain Sundays they would all wear the same color, the men sporting tuxedos and the women fancy, feathered hats. At first this finery perplexed me. I knew many arrived in poor cars. I assumed some lived in the nearby tiny houses that had once been slave cottages. I came to realize that clothing is a rather affordable means of personal pride.

My sister and I show personal pride in different ways. Some things important to her self-image and pride I call luxuries because I don't value or choose them. On the other hand, my sister has supplemented her income by cleaning houses, something I would loathe to do. It is all a difference of value and pride. Today I made an infrequent visit to one of the nicer groceries in town. Prices there are higher than I am willing to pay, but I wanted a bouquet of flowers. To my surprise, I saw someone who had come to the food pantry because they were out of food. I thought critically, "Why is she shopping here?"

It could be she does not have a car, and this grocery is the shortest walk; but it could also be a matter of personal pride. I wonder if after experiencing the humiliation of purchasing groceries each month with food stamps, she feels a need to spend her few other dollars at the "nice" grocery. I wonder if she feels more like a valued person when she presents her Valued Customer Card and has her groceries packed and carried to the car. If so, paying a few cents more per item may be a bargain boost to her self-esteem.

Thoughts on 11th Street

Last winter, driving down 11th Street, I came close to hitting a man walking on the side of the road. He staggered and almost fell into the path of my car. I realized he was intoxicated or high on drugs. I wondered where he had gotten the money for the alcohol or drugs. A friend of mine told me that before her husband conquered his alcoholism, he had spent $200 a month or more on beer. But how had this poorly dressed man paid for alcohol or drugs? Had he sold the winter coat a helping agency gave him? Or worse, had he sold his children's coats and Christmas presents? Perhaps he had gotten a food order from one of the pantries, maybe even including my fresh garden vegetables, and sold half of it for booze. My mind was flooded with resentments.

Then my mind switched to our three burglaries. We think my grandmother's wedding ring and my mother's engagement ring and many other memories went to buy drugs for a troubled neighbor. I felt again the helpless violation. Undoubtedly I would much rather my personal charity be taken advantage of than my home invaded and my fears aroused. It is more cost effective to misuse our social justice system than to use our criminal justice system. So if I should see the man I nearly harmed at the food pantry, I will greet him with a welcoming smile, knowing he is an addict or alcoholic. If he uses his food order for nourishment, then it might be giving his body the strength to fight its addiction. If he sells the food for drugs or booze, then, wrong as that is, at least it is not the illegal violation of someone's treasures.

Black Plastic

The way we are able to manage a garden as big as ours is with the liberal use of black plastic. When we plant, we alternate the plants with plastic: a row of beans, a length of plastic, a row of tomatoes, another length of plastic. The plastic holds the moisture, keeps the soil warm, gives people a place to walk, and, most importantly, keeps the weeds down. It means we only weed right around the plants themselves.

Rob says our black plastic is the superego of the garden, controlling the id (weeds), so the ego (vegetables) can flourish. That is clearly a psychology major talking!

I tend to think of the black plastic as the moral standards of the garden. The only real purpose for holding moral standards is to allow us to pre-decide choices before we are faced with the actual situations. In fact, holding moral standards tends to keep us out of situations in which we might be tempted to make choices we would later regret.

It worries me that many young people believe that there is no right and no wrong, only situations. That seems to me to be like trying to pull out the weeds in the whole garden, resulting in a great deal of time and effort. Using black plastic blocks out large areas where no weeds grow, allowing the gardener to concentrate the weeding where it is needed. Likewise, using moral standards blocks out whole areas of temptation, allowing us to concentrate our choices in areas of greatest concern.

Gardening Pants

My favorite pair of gardening pants has a big split in the knee. I wear them anyway, but I notice my kneecap is looking decidedly darkened with ground-in dirt. Reluctantly, I commit my pants to the rag bin. One of life's frustrating realities is that my favorite clothes wear out, but the clothes I care little about hang around looking new in my closet for years.

When my mother died, I was amazed to find in her closet a pair of shoes that she had worn when I was a child. They must not have fit quite right and thus never wore out sufficiently to get rid of them. Ironically, they have become one of my favorite pairs, and I have put more wear on them in three years than Mom did in thirty. I have those nearly new derelicts in my closet, too: the army-green blouse, the skirt with the wavy hem, the suit that is difficult to iron. Having difficulty finding clothes to fit my six-foot body, I am reluctant to part with anything that fits, even if I never wear it. The derelicts simply hang there representing poor choices that never go away.

Choices and actions in the past cannot be undone. They just hang around in our memory, evoking a flash of emotion. Why do I still worry about the 1974 health club membership I bought and used only once? Or why can the thought of a twenty-year-old goof still make me blush with embarrassment? I have decided to take my unworn clothes to the church garage sale. What I really need is a garage sale for my memory, a place to rid myself of past bad choices. I realize such a garage sale exists: It is called "forgiveness." Perhaps in time, I will learn to forgive my mistakes.

Pumpkin

A volunteer pumpkin is growing in the corner of the garden. It came up quietly and began to claim its spot. Interestingly enough, it has grown straight down our last row of black plastic, turning neither to the left nor to the right. It grows by some mysterious guide. I admire this unplanned visitor to our garden that exudes purpose and confidence as it sprouts giant leaves on its straight stem. I similarly admire people who show self-assurance and drive, who know exactly who they are and where they are heading. I do not know such certainty. I often wonder which way I am called to go and whether my life is what God intended in giving me my gifts. I worry, "How I can launch my child into a happy, purposeful life when I cannot find my own clear path?"

Today I went out to the garden to discover my pumpkin had disappeared. I dug down into the crabgrass and found its remnants withered and dead. How could this happen? True, we have never succeeded in growing pumpkins, but this plant seemed so healthy, so full of destiny. How could it have died so quickly? Did a cutworm or squash borer attack it? Or did it die because no other pumpkin was near enough to exchange pollen?

Whatever the reason, I mourn this passing of a symbol. However, it has set me wondering if perhaps nothing in life is certain. Perhaps other people only seem more directed and purposeful. Perhaps uncertainly is always the companion of commitment.

Wildflowers

Every year around the end of July, Andrew and I make a big bouquet of wildflowers for Sunday worship at our church. They are dedicated to my parents. My mother made many such bouquets when I was growing up. I spent most of my growing-up years in central Illinois, but like many young people, I was eager to leave and determined never to return. After leaving for college in Texas, graduate school in Vermont, and young married life in New York City, I came to deny that I was "from" anywhere in particular. If asked, I would reply, "Oh, I've lived a lot of different places." Meanwhile, my parents retired and moved away from the "land of Lincoln." So for many years I did not return to this state.

A cross-country trip brought me back to Illinois. As we traveled through, I found myself looking eagerly at the roadside scene, inspecting the crops, and enjoying the flat vistas. But what really turned my head were the wildflowers along the side of the road: Queen Anne's lace, red clover, purple thistles, brown-eyed Susans, cornflowers, and blue chicory. Accenting the flowers were brown dock and wild dill and the wispy tan grasses topped by bushy ticklers. It was all very familiar.

The wildflowers showed me that I did have a "home place," somewhere to be from. It was central Illinois. No matter how far I have traveled, this is the place whose familiarity resonates with my soul. Life has brought me back to live in Illinois; and, once a year, I gather the wildflowers from the roadside as a worthy tribute to my upbringing.

third season

Heat

It's only late July, but the garden looks like late August or even late September. The plants are simply worn out. Some of the tomato plants are turning brown and dying, although their tomatoes are still small and green. The cucumbers and peppers are misshapen and splotchy. Why this exhaustion? It is because of the high heat we've experienced this summer. Our air conditioner has run almost continually since the second week of June. Temperatures have not dipped below 90 degrees for three weeks, and one week reached 100+ temperatures for four days in a row. The air itself feels hot to breathe, and even the beach is deserted. We've had frequent thunderstorms, so the ground is not dry, but nevertheless the plants are brown— simply baked by heat.

I think heat is much like stress. Vegetables need hot summer weather to grow. They need bright sunshine, warm soil, and temperate nights. But unrelenting high heat saps their life and wears them out. So it is with stress. The stress of change or challenge often sparks our life and makes it interesting. However, the stress of long-term anger, grief, or pain saps our life and wears us down. Today I have felt so sapped.

But the garden encourages me, for I know the heat cannot last; cool weather will come with fall. Then, even if this gardening season is marred and unproductive, a new spring will come with the new chance for growth. In the same way, my mood will lift, and the seasons of my life will change.

Iced Coffee

Today promises to be incredibly hot, as it has been for many days now. Jerie and I, by unspoken agreement, met at the garden very early this morning. Even so, the temperature was high, and the air felt heavy. We got the buckets from the shed and waded in to pick the cucumbers, squash, and green beans. All too soon we needed a break in the shade. Then we returned to seek out the broccoli and the turnips. Weeds poke their heads up everywhere, but it is simply too hot for us to give them any attention. We carried our produce to the house and were met at the door by a welcome blast of air conditioning. Ahh! The morning was still young, but we felt limp and spent. "Do you want an iced coffee?" I asked. "Sure, that sounds great," nodded Jerie. Quickly, the glasses were filled, and we sat in the kitchen sipping our cold drinks and talking in the easy way of good friends.

It amazes me how certain tastes or smells can bring back vivid memories. Years ago, when my college roommate and I were traveling around Europe, we found ourselves in Florence, Italy, when the temperature was 40° C. (That's over 100° F.) Undaunted, we set out to see the sights. About midday we stumbled down some steps into a dark basement bar. The waitress looked us over and without asking for our order returned with two, tall, iced coffees. I had never drunk iced coffee before, but on that day, it tasted wonderful. We spent the rest of the scorching afternoon sitting, talking quietly, and drinking iced coffee. Today again, iced coffee had the wonderful taste of cool refreshment and good friendship.

third season

Tomatoes 1

This week we picked our first few tomatoes. Unfortunately they have crusty brown blemishes. I sliced them for lunch, a bit dubious of their flavor. We were delighted to taste the wonderful sweet goodness of tomatoes fresh from the garden, the taste we have waited for.

This morning's mail brought an advertisement urging us to buy a loose-leaf gardening book. Sample pages were included. Being curious, I picked up the page for tomatoes. The sheet advised me that splits in tomatoes are caused by uneven watering: dry conditions followed by too much water. Furthermore, I was warned to avoid blemishes by protecting my tomatoes from heat and wind.

Hmmm…Sounds like I'm to keep my tomatoes away from Illinois summers, hot dry weather punctuated by drenching thunderstorms. The book seems to suggest that the best place to grow tomatoes is a greenhouse. Unfortunately, we all know hothouse tomatoes lack flavor. They seem neither sweet nor sour, but are just flat in taste.

I think the same is true in life. People often wish to shield themselves and their children from struggles and trials. But struggling builds strength, both of muscle and character. If we were to manage to live a life devoid of pain, grief, hardship, or challenge, then I think we would find we were living a life devoid of empathy, understanding, wisdom, and triumph. In short, it would be a life rather flat in flavor.

Tomatoes 2

Our seeds and seedlings from the Illinois Hunger Coalition offer us a grab bag. The tags give only the generic name—beans or radishes—not indicating a particular kind. We got two flats of tomatoes containing different varieties. The seedlings of one were short, compact, and dark green; the others were tall, stringy, and olive in color. Now they are producing, and the difference is even more striking. One kind has round, smooth, and bright-orange tomatoes. Rob says they look like tomatoes should look. Unfortunately many of these have big white spots of sunburn and split skins.

The second variety has tomatoes of a pink color with tops that stay green even when ripe. They are rather flat and knobby and have a brown crusty spot at the bottom. Because of their shape and blemishes, they cannot be sliced into nice tomato rounds. However, this kind is surviving the hot sun, despite its odd appearance. For fun, we decided to have the tomato challenge and see which variety tasted best. Despite their very different looks, they taste almost the same—like fresh, garden-ripe tomatoes. I guess the labels were right. Despite their obvious differences, they are still basically "tomatoes."

I wish each of us would come with a plain label that says "person." Too often we divide people by their appearance and trappings; we divide them into a wide number of varieties and categories. We forget that, despite our race, age, religion, occupation, gender, nationality, or finances, we are all essentially the same: "persons" and children of God.

Nightmares

During the night, my dreams were filled with anxiety and unfinished business. About 4:00 a.m., I woke up, covered with sweat. I went downstairs for a drink of milk and a cookie. That helped settle me down, but it didn't send me back to sleep.

This morning we are leaving on vacation and will be gone for ten days. These last few days I've had a list of things to remember and accomplish before we left. Most of them are done, but during the night my subconscious resurrected several other tasks that I had left undone.

At 5:00, I gave up on sleep, got up, and headed for the computer. Three letters later, and a call to a business answering machine, I was finished and ready to get dressed, pack the car, and go on vacation.

Despite the early hour and my shortened sleep, I am surprisingly refreshed. Apparently my body is more lightened by the relief of anxiety than by the length of sleep. I believe it is actually my soul that is lightened. I must remember the next time I have anxious nightmares or lie awake worrying that if I can get up and relieve my soul, my body will be rested as well.

Back to Routine

This morning I trudged out to the garden for our Saturday picking for the first time in three weekends. We were on vacation the last two Saturdays, and Jerie took care of the harvest. Then all this past week I have only glanced out at the garden. The sight of my zinnias barely lifting their heads above the crabgrass repelled me and made me keep my distance. While away we got a chance to change our pace: to camp, build fires, and lay in the hammock; to sightsee and swim and do little or nothing. But while we were "getting away," someone broke into our house and "got away" with some of our possessions. So we returned from our good experience to face a bad experience.

Both the very good and the very bad can rob us of the rhythm of daily life. Frequently we hear the advice, "Time to get back to work" or "You'll just have to pick up where you left off." How difficult that advice is to follow. Experiences, whether good or bad, affect and change us. They make it hard for us to go back to doing everything the same as before. In addition, while we are distracted, life around us moves on. My garden exemplifies this. I have found it very hard to step back into the garden routine. I missed Wednesday night's picking and only reluctantly returned today. Plus, while I was both physically and mentally away, the garden has changed. The winter squash and tomatoes have ripened, the zucchini has died, and the crabgrass has exploded.

I cannot simply pick up where I left the garden before our vacation and our burglary. I have changed, and the garden has changed as well.

Sunburn

I have a bad sunburn. I didn't get it in the garden. I know better than that. I got it at a water park where I took Andrew and his friend Helen. We stayed long enough to get our money's worth…and got more than enough sun.

The only parts of me—not covered by my swimsuit—that have escaped redness are my already-darkened gardener's hands. While in the garden, I usually wear long sleeves, long pants, and a hat, leaving only my hands exposed.

When I was growing up, it was interesting to see the farmers in their fields. The teenagers went shirtless and hatless, sporting a chocolate color. Their fathers wore short-sleeved T-shirts and baseball caps. Their grandfathers wore long-sleeved flannel shirts and wide-brim straw hats. With growing age, the farmers increasingly protected themselves from the rays of the sun.

I can relate. Today, as I look at my sunburned face and body, all the flaws and wrinkles seem enhanced. I remember when a tan made me look healthy and vital. Now, it only seems to make me look old and worn.

Many things are like that. Things that sounded exciting and romantic and adventuresome as a teen now arouse my fears and sense of frailty: Mountain climbing, carnival rides, and African safaris no longer appeal.

However, occasionally we must head out on a new adventure. But then I must expect sore muscles, weary feet, or sunburn to remind me that my body and my dreams are no longer young.

Break in the Weather

The extreme heat this summer has been hard on gardens and gardeners alike. Yesterday, I turned off the air conditioning and opened the windows for the first time in months. We've decided to close down most of the garden early. Although the calendar says early September, the garden looks like late October. The harvest is slim, and the weeds are now in violation of the city ordinance.

Last night was a cool, breezy, pleasant evening. My friend Jan came over, and together we spent the evening pulling up tomato plants and stacking cages. As we talked about how poor our gardens had been, we enjoyed the companionship and the relief of pulling up the source of our disappointment. This morning Jerie and Rob and I met in the garden—all smiles. We yanked out the rest of the tomatoes, gathered the squash vines, and pulled up the black plastic. Finally, we took a weed eater to our crabgrass. We spent the morning renovating the garden, changing it from waste and weeds to a clear plot containing only green peppers and flowers. After two hours of fun, we stood back admiring our work. It felt like spring again when the air is cool and the ground is bare.

After such a disappointing growing season, it was a time to get a fresh view, to find again pleasure in the garden, and to rediscover why we are gardeners. The cool air brought that opportunity. I pray that every time my life goes through a time of searing heat and disappointment, a cool breeze will help renew my purpose.

Fall Lettuce

This morning Jerie and I tilled the earth and planted spinach, lettuce, and radishes. The air was cool, and we laughed and talked as we dug the ground and planted the seed. It reminded me of spring again, but there is a difference…It is fall.

Last week, disappointed at our garden's poor performance, we cleared the ground of almost everything. This clearing suddenly left both time and space to grow a fall garden.

I've never grown a fall garden before. Usually the time to plant comes and goes with us busily picking baskets of tomatoes. In fact, this opportunity has come about only because of the failure of our main crop.

I once heard a saying, "When God closes a door, God opens a window." Losses and failures leave a space for new understandings and new purpose. While we were experiencing the heat of this summer and worrying over our baked plants, we didn't think about a fall garden. Only after we had cleared away the old plants and made the ground barren did the notion occur to plant again.

Fall Radishes

This evening I discovered the first fall radishes are ready to eat. The lettuce sports a splash of bright spring green, and the little "V" sprouts of spinach have grown leaves. The weather is cool and sunny, ideal for these plants to thrive. Even the night frost has stayed away, as each day has been picture-perfect. The whole garden seems to be rejuvenated. The green peppers are blooming, the nasturtiums are blanketed with flowers, one remaining broccoli plant is filled with new spears, and green onions are reappearing. As Jerie said, "Everything seems to be trying to compensate." Although I know that frost will soon come, I carry my radishes to the house and fantasize about having a spinach-and-lettuce salad for Thanksgiving.

The last two seasons we have ended our efforts with the closing of the garden and with thanksgiving for the abundant harvest. This third season seemed likely to end in disappointment and wilted hopes, as the garden was baked brown under the searing sun; but here in the small row of new radishes is the joy of beginning again. We ask God for blessing on these new sprouts and give thanks for the continuing blessings in our life.

> You have turned my mourning into dancing;
>   you have taken off my sackcloth
>   and clothed me with joy,
> so that my soul may praise you and not be silent.
>   O LORD my God, I will give thanks to you forever.
>
> PSALM 30:11–12

Many things have happened in our lives since I first wrote down these thoughts. The most obvious changes have occurred for our son, Andrew, who was six, seven, and eight when these lines were written. He has now passed both his parents in height, wears a size 13 shoe, and has headed for college. He was a boy who filled our lives with gladness, and he is now a man who fills our hearts with pride.

But other things have changed in our lives. After six years of planting our garden as a hunger garden, we moved from that home to a house without a garden plot. However, it was a ministry that we were not sad to leave, because an amazing thing had occurred at our food pantry: many persons had followed our lead. As Carolyn said, "We look like Farmers' Market here with all our fresh vegetables." Somehow the garden ministry had spread, so that when we brought our vegetables into Kulmer Church, the table was already filled with produce from other gardens. Neither we, nor the staff there, quite know how this wealth of fresh food came about. Quietly the word spread about our garden, and other gardeners followed.

I always liked the story of the feeding of the 5,000. The little boy who innocently offered his lunch to Jesus could not have known the possibility that lay within those few fish and loaves when placed in God's hands. When we offered our garden to God, we had no idea either of the bountiful harvest we would receive or of the extent to which God would use and multiply our offering.

This book is much like my garden. When I plant and tend a seed, the effort on my part is small compared to the use God makes of that seed through the power of creation. Likewise, God has taken my scribblings on a yellow pad and sent them out to touch people's lives. A cancer patient received a copy from her pastor, and she asked for a dozen copies to give to her supporting friends after her death. Another man took a copy home to his wife. He later called to ask if he might till our garden as a gift. The night he came to till, he quietly shared with us that his wife suffered from deep, chronic depression. Although at one time she had loved books, she had not been able to read a book in four years. He said, "She was able to read your book, not once, but twice, and I thank you."

Among the lives most touched has been my own, for I have never felt so strongly God's work and leading in my life as through my little books. Since their writing, I entered and finished seminary, and have become a hospice chaplain.

I hope that this book has opened some doors of thought for you. I hope that you have found some favorite essays—ones that particularly spoke to you. I hope my musings have encouraged you to see the richness in your own life, the value of the small daily happenings. Finally, I hope that you find a way in your own life to touch nature and participate in God's ongoing creation.

Good gardening to you,
Dori Dana Hudson